Teaching With Dear America Books

by Jeannette Sanderson

SCHOLASTIC
PROFESSIONAL BOOKS

New York • Toronto • London • Auckland • Sydney
Mexico City • New Delhi • Hong Kong • Buenos Aires

For my editors,
Virginia Dooley and Mela Ottaiano

For a complete list of Dear America and My Name Is America titles,
visit our Web site at www.scholastic.com or call 1-800-724-6527.

Scholastic Inc. grants teachers permission to photocopy the designated reproducible pages from this book for classroom use.
No other part of this publication may be reproduced in whole or in part, or stored in a retrieval system, or transmitted in any form or
by any means, electronic, mechanical, photocopying, recording, or otherwise, without written permission of the publisher.
For information regarding permission, write to Scholastic Inc., 555 Broadway, New York, NY 10012.

DEAR AMERICA®, SCHOLASTIC, and associated logos are trademarks and/or registered trademarks of Scholastic Inc.

Cover design by Josué Castilleja
Cover image: Library of Congress
Interior design by Sydney Wright
Maps by Jim McMahon

ISBN 0-439-10547-1

Copyright © 2001 by Jeannette Sanderson. All rights reserved.
Printed in the U.S.A.

Table of Contents

Introduction

One of the best ways to interest children in history is to present it to them through the eyes of a child. That is what the Dear America books do. Once that interest is piqued, however, it is up to you, the teacher, to take advantage of it. *Teaching With Dear America Books* is designed to help you do just that, providing guides for 12 popular Dear America books that cover American history from colonial times through immigration in the early 1900s.

The book is divided into five sections—one for each time period: Colonial America, the Revolutionary War, Westward Expansion, the Civil War, and Immigration. Each section begins with a time line of important events and includes teaching guides for two or more books. Every teaching guide includes a brief summary of the book, glossary, and discussion cues intended to help activate students' prior knowledge about the book's subject and historical context. There are also questions, activities, and a reproducible that extend students' understanding. Finally, each section ends with discussion questions and activities to help students compare and contrast the books and develop a better understanding of certain aspects of life during that period in American history.

Many children—and adults—think history is just a list of names and dates to be memorized then forgotten. Using this book in conjunction with its related titles from the Dear America series will help you show students the bigger picture; that history is the story of how real people have lived and died during much of the last four centuries in America. This book will also help you meet the English Language Arts and Social Studies standards shown below.

∼ MEETING ENGLISH LANGUAGE ARTS STANDARDS ∼

◆ Students apply a wide range of strategies to comprehend, interpret, evaluate, and appreciate texts. They draw on their prior experience, their interactions with other readers and writers, their knowledge of word meaning and of other texts, their word identification strategies, and their understanding of textual features (e.g., sound-letter correspondence, sentence structure, context, graphics).

◆ Students employ a wide range of strategies as they write and use different writing process elements appropriately to communicate with different audiences for a variety of purposes.

◆ Students use a variety of technological and information resources (e.g., libraries, databases, computer networks, video) to gather and synthesize information and to create and communicate knowledge.

◆ Students develop an understanding of and respect for diversity in language use, patterns, and dialects across cultures, ethnic groups, geographic regions, and social roles.

◆ Students participate as knowledgeable, reflective, creative, and critical members of literacy communities.

Standards developed by NCTE and IRA

◆ *Culture* The study of culture prepares students to answer questions such as: What are the common characteristics of different cultures? How do belief systems, such as religion or political ideals, influence other parts of the culture? How does the culture change to accommodate different ideas and beliefs? What does language tell us about the culture?

◆ *Time, Continuity, and Change*
Human beings seek to understand their historical roots and to locate themselves in time. Knowing how to read and reconstruct the past allows one to develop a historical perspective and to answer questions such as: Who am I? What happened in the past? How am I connected to those in the past? How has the world changed and how might it change in the future? Why does our personal sense of relatedness to the past change?

◆ *Individual Development and Identity* Personal identity is shaped by one's culture, by groups, and by institutional influences. Students should consider such questions as: How do people learn? Why do people behave as they do? What influences how people learn, perceive, and grow? How do people meet their basic needs in a variety of contexts? How do individuals develop from youth to adulthood?

◆ *Individuals, Groups, and Institutions* Institutions such as schools, churches, families, government agencies, and the courts play an integral role in people's lives. It is important that students learn how institutions are formed, what controls and influences them, how they influence individuals and culture, and how they are maintained or changed. Students may address questions such as: What is the role of institutions in this and other societies? How am I influenced by institutions? How do institutions change? What is my role in institutional change?

◆ *Power, Authority, and Governance*
Understanding the historical development of structures of power, authority, and governance and their evolving functions in contemporary U.S. society and other parts of the world is essential for developing civic competence. In exploring this theme, students confront questions such as: What is power? What forms does it take? Who holds it? How is it gained, used, and justified? What is legitimate authority? How are governments created, structured, maintained, and changed? How can individual rights be protected within the context of majority rule?

◆ *Civic Ideals and Practices* An understanding of civic ideals and practices of citizenship is critical to full participation in society and is a central purpose of the social studies. Students confront such questions as: What is civic participation and how can I be involved? How has the meaning of citizenship evolved? What is the balance between rights and responsibilities? What is the role of the citizen in the community and the nation, and as a member of the world community? How can I make a positive difference?

Standards developed by NCSS

1513 Ponce de Leon claims Florida for Spain.

1565 Spain establishes a permanent settlement at St. Augustine, Florida.

1607 About 100 colonists settle Jamestown, Virginia, which becomes the first permanent English colony.

1609 Henry Hudson, in search of Northwest Passage, sails up the New York river that bears his name, claiming the area for the Dutch.

1610 Spain establishes a colony at Santa Fe (in present-day New Mexico).

1619 A Dutch ship brings 20 Africans to Jamestown, Virginia, where they become indentured servants.

The House of Burgesses, the first colonial legislature, meets in Jamestown, Virginia.

1620 The Pilgrims settle Plymouth, Massachusetts, after signing the Mayflower Compact, an agreement that established self-government.

1621 Several Native Americans—including Massasoit, a Wampanoag leader, and Squanto, a Patuxet—help the Pilgrims survive in their new land by teaching them such things as how to grow corn.

1624 The Dutch establish the settlement of New Netherland, which grows to include New Amsterdam (present-day New York City).

1626 Dutchman Peter Minuit purchases the island of Manhattan from the Manhattan Indians for about $24 worth of goods.

1630 John Winthrop and others found the Massachusetts Bay Colony, where about 20,000 people will settle by 1640.

1636 Roger Williams founds Providence, Rhode Island, after being expelled from Massachusetts for threatening the Puritan government there.

1644 Chief Opechancanough of the Powhatan Confederacy attacks the outlying settlements of Jamestown, killing more than 300. The colonists strike back and defeat the Native Americans.

1675-
1676 King Philip's War wipes out the Narragansett Indians, gradually subdues the Wampanoag and Nipmuck, and results in the virtual extermination of Native Americans in southern New England.

1676 Bacon's Rebellion—Virginia farmer Nathaniel Bacon and other Virginia colonists burn Jamestown in protest of the British government's failure to stop Native American raids on western settlements.

1680 The Pueblo revolt, forcing the Spanish to leave Santa Fe.

1681 English Quaker William Penn is granted a royal charter for the land that becomes Pennsylvania.

1682 France claims the Mississippi River Valley.

1723 The first permanent school for Native Americans is established in Williamsburg, Virginia.

1732 Georgia, the last of the 13 colonies, is settled.

1754-
1763 England and France fight the Seven Years' War, or French and Indian War, for control over North America. England wins.

1763 In an effort to prevent more wars, the British issue the Proclamation of 1763, which reserves the area west of the Appalachians for Native American nations and bars colonial settlement there. The order is ignored by many colonists.

A Journey to the New World

The Diary of Remember Patience Whipple

✦ **Summary** ✦ *A Journey to the New World: The Diary of Remember Patience Whipple* by Kathryn Lasky is the story of a twelve-year-old girl's voyage on the *Mayflower* and settlement in Plymouth Colony. Along with Mem, the reader journeys thousands of miles from Leyden (Leiden), Holland, to Plimoth (Plymouth), with stops at Southampton, England, and Cape Cod Bay. Mem measures her journey in miles, but there is another way to measure it—by her experiences and growth as a person. The young Pilgrim makes friends with people who are different. She watches loved ones, including her mother, die. She learns to judge people from their actions, not their words; to open her heart to new people; and to speak up for what she believes. She survives. And she grows into her name—Patience.

✦ **Prior Knowledge** ✦ Ask students what they know about the *Mayflower*. Where did the ship sail from? What was its destination? Who sailed on it? Why did these people leave their homes to sail to an unknown land? What was the journey like? Where did the ship land? When? What was it like settling in this new land? Who helped the settlers survive in their new home?

∼ GLOSSARY ∼

abate: become less intense

accord: peaceful agreement

adze: a cutting tool

allotment: something that is given out in shares

awl: a sharp metal tool for making holes in leather or wood

brazier: a pan for holding burning coals

cantankerous: difficult to deal with

coif: a close-fitting cap

compact: an agreement between people or groups

cross-staff: an instrument once used to measure the elevation of heavenly bodies

cuff: to hit with the palm of the hand

decoction: a boiled down extract

draught (Brit. version of draft): potion, especially one having medicinal powers

florid: reddish

gloaming: twilight, dusk

hardtack: a saltless hard biscuit or bread made of flour and water

headland: a point of land jutting out into a body of water

hillock: a small hill

incredulous: unable to believe something or accept that it is true

indentured servant: someone who worked without wages for a period of time in exchange for passage to the American colonies

laden: carrying a lot of things

pallet: a straw-filled mattress

parley: to speak with one another

pen nib: the sharpened point of a quill pen

pilgrims: religious travelers in a foreign land

pipkin: a small pot

pod: a small herd of animals, such as whales or seals

poppet: doll

privy: toilet

profane: with disregard for God

providence: divine guidance or care

provisions: supplies of food

quills: hollow shafts used in mechanical devices

rive: to split

Ruling Elder: a church officer or leader

Sabbath: the day of rest and worship in some religions

Saints of the Holy Disciple: what the Puritans who sailed on the *Mayflower* called themselves

saltpeter: a salty, white mineral used in making gunpowder

satchel: a small bag or suitcase

scours: diarrhea

scurvy: a disease caused by lack of vitamin C (ascorbic acid) in the diet that results in bleeding gums and great weakness

Separatists: a group of 16th and 17th century English Protestants preferring to separate from, rather than reform, the Church of England

shroud: a cloth used to wrap a dead body

Strangers: the name given by Separatists to those on the *Mayflower* traveling for other than religious reasons

sundry: various

vapors: exhalations once believed to be harmful to a person's health

vial: a small bottle for holding liquids

victuals: supplies of food

waistcoat: a short, sleeveless coat or vest

wampum: beads made from polished shells — strung together or woven to make belts, collars, and necklaces — used by some Native Americans as money

wigwam: a hut made of poles and covered with bark or hides

SAILING GLOSSARY

bow: the front of a ship

cabin: a private room on a ship

courses: the lowest sails on a square-rigged mast

crosswinds: winds blowing in directions not parallel to a course

crow's nest: a partly enclosed platform high on a ship's mast, for use as a lookout

current: the movement of water in a river or an ocean

deck: the floor of a boat or ship

first mate: a ship's officer

footrope: the part of a rope sewn to the lower edge of a sail for reinforcement

forecastle: a raised deck near the bow of a ship

gale: very strong wind

galley: the ship's kitchen

halyard: rope used for raising and lowering sails

hatch: a covered hole in the deck

helmsman: the person steering the ship

hull: the frame or body of the ship

larder: a small room or pantry where the food is stored

longboat: the largest boat carried by a merchant sailing ship

lookout: the person who keeps watch

luff: to turn the head of a ship towards the wind

main beam: the main horizontal supporting piece of wood on a ship

mast: a tall pole that stands on the deck of a boat or ship and supports its sails

mizzen: a mast behind the ship's mainmast

mutiny: a revolt against the person or persons in charge

poop deck: a short raised deck at the rear of a ship

port: the left side of a ship

quartermaster: a petty officer in charge of the navigation devices on a ship

ratlines: small ropes that form a ladder on the ship's mast

rigging: the ropes and wires on a ship that support and control the sails

round house: a cabin on the back area of a ship's upper deck

sea charts: maps

shallop: a small, light, open boat with sail or oars

starboard: the right side of a ship

stateroom: a private room on a ship with sleeping facilities

steerage: the part of a ship occupied by passengers paying the lowest rate

stern: the back end of a ship

topsail: the sail next above the lowermost sail on a mast in a square-rigged ship

topside: the upper part of a ship, especially above the water line

turbulent: wild, not calm or smooth

weigh anchor: to lift an anchor in preparation for sailing

~ DISCUSSION QUESTIONS ~

Taking Risks for Justice King James of England swore vengeance on anyone connected with printing church books that spoke out against him and the Bishops, yet Mem's father agreed to help fix a printing press that printed such books. (page 13) *Would you have agreed to help? What do Mem's father's actions say about him? How much would you be willing to risk for what you believe?*

What's in a Name? William Bradford calls all the people who sail aboard the *Mayflower* "pilgrims." Mem likes the thought of Hummy and herself "no longer just being Saint and Stranger. For those two words doth pull us apart. 'Tis better to find a word that brings us together and might fit us both." (page 18) *Think of how names and labels are used today. What are some examples of names that divide and names that unite?*

A Woman's Place "It is most uncommon, unheard of, for a woman to speak out thusly," Mem wrote after her mother told Elder Brewster that his conversation was not suited for children. (page 20) *What do Mem's words say about the position of women at the time? What do her mother's actions tell you about what kind of person she was?*

Safe or Sorry? William and Dorothy Bradford feared for their son's safety on the *Mayflower*, so they left him in Holland. Mem writes, "I would think I should rather die" than be left behind by her mother and father. (page 25) *Imagine you are a parent preparing to make a long and dangerous journey to the New World. Would you bring your child with you or leave him or her behind? As a child, would you rather be left safely at home or go with your parents despite the risks? Give reasons for your answers.*

Facing Your Fears Mem writes, "I do not like the shadows of fears lurking about. I shall bring them into the light" by writing about them. (page 28) *In your experience, is it better to face your fears or ignore them? Mem writes about her fears. How do you face your fears?*

Is Wrong Ever Right? When Mem's friend Will is very sick, she and Hummy agree to steal Deacon Fuller's draught. (page 31) *Are Mem and Hummy right to plan to steal medicine for Will? Is it ever right to steal? Explain your answer.*

A Long Journey It took 65 days for the *Mayflower* to reach the New World. (page 39) *Make a list of some of the things you have done during the last 65 days. Can you imagine spending that much time in a crowded ship? How well do you think you would have survived the journey? What, if anything, would ever lead you to take such a long, dangerous journey to an unknown land?*

Looking Out for Others When Mem sees Dorothy Bradford grieving at the ship's rail she considers trying to comfort her but decides not to disturb her. Then when the grieving woman falls overboard, Mem writes, "I cannot stop wondering if I somehow could have stopped all this." (page 66) *What would you have done in Mem's shoes—tried to comfort Mrs. Bradford or let her be? Do you think Mem is in any way responsible for Mrs. Bradford's death? Why or why not?*

Missing Mother Several months after her mother's death, Mem writes, "I wonder if one ever grows old enough not to miss her mother." (page 127) *Do you think a person ever grows old enough not to miss her or his mother?*

Patience Mem's full name is Remember Patience Whipple. Throughout the book she often bemoans her lack of patience. *Give several examples of when Mem had to be patient. Give an example of when you've had to be patient. Do you find being patient easy or difficult?*

~ ACTIVITIES ~

Dear Diary Refer students to page 13 where Mem describes how her mother made her the diary she now uses. Ask students to make their own diaries or journals. They can be as simple (construction paper covers stapled over plain paper) or as elaborate (fabric-covered cardboard covers over plain paper bound with ribbon) as you like. Discuss with students the benefits of keeping a diary (for example, having a place to express yourself freely, face your fears, work out problems, and record events for future reference). Then provide time each day for students to write in their diaries. Stress that these are private, although students who wish to share from them may do so.

Classroom Compact Discuss the Mayflower Compact with students. Explain that this document, considered to be the first written constitution in North America, was the Pilgrims' statement of self-government. In it, the signers agreed "to enact, constitute, and frame such just and equall lawes, ordinances, acts, constitutions, and offices . . . as shall be thought most meete and convenient for the generall good of the Colonie, unto which we promise all due submission and obedience." Ask students to write a "classroom compact"—a set of class rules for the good of all.

Naming Names In *A Journey to the New World*, Mem writes, "I do feel that one of the finest things about coming into this New World is that we can become namers of places . . . ." (page 68) Ask students to imagine that they are the first people to live where they do. Ask them to use their imaginations to think of new names for streets, lakes, rivers, mountains, and other places that they find around them.

The First Thanksgiving Ask students to draw a picture of the first Thanksgiving based on Mem's descriptions of it. (pages 145–147)

Meet the Pilgrims Have students learn more about the Pilgrims and Plimoth Plantation by visiting the Plimoth Plantation Web site at http://www.pilgrims.net/plymouth/.

Answers for Mem's Journey
1. c 2. a 3. a 4. b 5. c Bonus: 42° north and 71° west

Mem's Journey

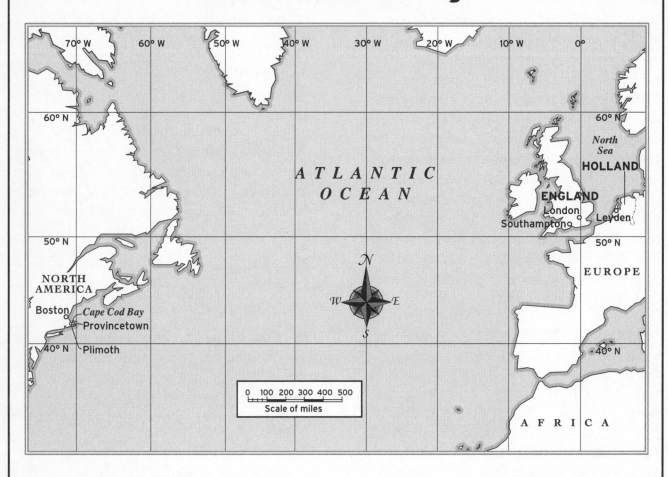

This map shows the important points in Mem's journey to the New World. Use the map key and the latitude/longitude grid to answer the questions.

1. About how far did Mem and her family have to travel to get from Leyden (Leiden), Holland, to Southampton, England?

Ⓐ 100 miles Ⓑ 200 miles Ⓒ 300 miles

2. Mem writes that she sailed 2950 miles on the *Mayflower* before she saw land. Using the scale of miles on this map, about how far is it from Southampton to Cape Cod Bay?

Ⓐ 2800 miles Ⓑ 3400 miles Ⓒ 4000 miles

3. What direction did the *Mayflower* sail to get from Southampton to Cape Cod Bay?

Ⓐ southwest Ⓑ northwest Ⓒ west

4. What is the approximate distance between Provincetown, where the *Mayflower* first landed, to Plimoth (Plymouth), where Mem and the others finally settled?

Ⓐ 5 miles Ⓑ 25 miles Ⓒ 75 miles

5. What place on Mem's journey was closest to the 50° north parallel?

Ⓐ Leyden Ⓑ London Ⓒ Southampton

Bonus: What is the approximate latitude and longitude of where the Pilgrims finally settled? _____

Standing in the Light

The Captive Diary of Catharine Carey Logan

♦ Summary ♦ *Standing in the Light: The Captive Diary of Catharine Carey Logan* by Mary Pope Osborne is the story of a thirteen-year-old Quaker girl's capture by the Lenape Indians, her nine months in captivity, and her eventual return to her mother and father. During her captivity, Caty learns to think of the Lenape as people, not savages. She grows to love them as her family. The experience transforms Caty from a child who worries a great deal what others think to a young woman who grows to trust her own judgment. It is the story of a girl who learns what is right—who learns to stand in the light.

♦ Prior Knowledge ♦ Ask students what they know about life in the 1760s. What was it like living where settlers and Native Americans were fighting over land? What did the colonists think of Native Americans then? What might it have been like to be captured? Also ask, who are the Quakers? What are their beliefs?

∼ GLOSSARY ∼

anguish: great mental pain, a strong feeling of misery or distress

britches: pants, trousers

card wool: to fasten wool on a card, an instrument for cleansing, separating, and collecting fibers

catechism: oral instruction

chasten: cause to be less proud

colicky: suffering from sharp stomach pain

copybook: a book used to teach penmanship

despair: to lose hope completely

devotions: prayer

encroachment: anything taken away by trespassing upon the property or rights of another

exile: forced removal from one's country or home

forsake: abandon

Friend: member of the Religious Society of Friends (see Quaker)

gruel: a thin porridge

heathen: a person who does not believe in the God of Christianity, Judaism, or Islam

humbled: made less proud

impudent: rude, bold, and outspoken

johnnycake: bread made with cornmeal

longhouse: a long home shared by several people

meeting house: a building used for public assembly and worship

melancholy: very sad

Moravian: a member of a Christian group that originated in a 15th century religious reform movement in Bohemia and Moravia

perpetual: without ending or changing

persecution: cruel and unfair treatment, especially of those who differ in origin, religion, or social outlook

poultice: a soft, moist mass of cloth, bread, meal, or herbs that is applied hot to the body as medicine

pungent: having a strong or sharp taste or smell

Quaker: a member of the Religous Society of Friends, a religious body founded in the middle of the 17th century that prefers simple religious services and opposes war

scorn: to reject or refuse with contempt or disdain

venison: deer meat

venomous: spiteful, malevolent

whooping cough: an infectious disease that makes children and babies cough violently and breathe noisily

~ DISCUSSION QUESTIONS ~

Extravagant Day's Walk In the Extravagant Day's Walk, the English took advantage of an agreement with the Delaware Indians that said they could have all the land they could walk on in one and a half days. They did this by cutting a path through the forest and hiring expert runners to run, rather than walk, the path. *How did the Delaware feel about this? Do you think they were right to feel betrayed? Do you think the English were right to do whatever they could to claim as much land as possible? What would you have done in their position? How would you have felt if you were one of the Delaware?*

Goodness and Happiness Caty writes that her father "believes that doing good will always help one's spirit." (page 17) *Do you agree? Can you think of a time when helping someone made you feel better?*

The Courage to Speak When Caty's schoolmates discuss the Native Americans and call them savages, Caty says, "I wanted to say what Papa had told me . . . but such a speech would have been too bold for me." (page 18) *Would you have spoken up and defended the Native Americans if you were Caty? Why or why not? Have you ever been in a situation similar to Caty's, when you felt you should have spoken up? Did you? Why or why not?*

Her Brother's Keeper After Caty and Thomas are captured, Caty writes, "I would try to escape, but Thomas is too weak to run with me. I will die before I forsake him." (pages 42–43) *What would you do if you were in Caty's shoes? Would you try to escape even if you had to leave your brother behind, or would you stay with your brother?*

A Savage Child The Native American baby makes Caty think of her sickly baby brother, Will. She writes, "Forgive me, Papa, but I wonder bitterly why God dost make this savage child more healthy and happy than His own Christian baby." (page 47) *Why is Caty asking her father's forgiveness? What do her words say about her feelings toward the Native Americans? How do her feelings change by the end of the book?*

Writing for Her Life Writing in her diary is so important to Caty that she writes, "What will I do, Papa? This is the last of my ink. Now for certain, I will totally disappear." (page 55) *Why was Caty's writing so important to her, especially after she was abducted? In what way do you think she felt she would disappear after her ink ran out?*

What Do Others Think? When Caty finds she is "turned out of herself," shouting and exclaiming, she asks, "Is it because I do not care any more what others think?" (page 56) *Do you think it should matter what other people think? How much does it matter to you? How can caring what others think help society? How can it be harmful?*

An Eye for an Eye Caty and her brother are kidnapped and given to White Owl and Black Snake because both had lost children to measles, a disease brought to America by Europeans. *Do you think the Native Americans had a right to kidnap Caty and her brother in exchange for the two children that they had lost to a European disease? Why or why not?*

Practice What You Preach Snow Hunter says to Caty, "I scorn you because you do not think of the Lenape as fellow creatures . . . . You preach love while all the time you think you are better than all people." (page 75) *Are Snow Hunter's words true? Do people always practice what they preach? Why not? In what ways do you practice what you preach? In what ways do you fall short?*

Truth, Not Victory Caty's father tells her, "It is *truth* we must strive for, not *victory*." (page 34) Later, when Black Snake lets Thomas be with Caty, she says, "Papa, in that moment, I could see it was *truth* they strived for, not *victory*." (page 89) *Do you agree with Caty's father that it is more important to strive for truth than victory? Why or why not? Is it possible to have both truth and victory?*

Two Families? As Caty comes to know and love White Owl, Little Cloud, and Little One, she begins to think of them as her new family. And yet she can't stand to think that she will never see her father, mother, Eliza, and Baby Will again. (page 123) *Imagine you are in Caty's situation. What do you think you would do? Would you try to accept your new family and forget about your old one? Would you keep your distance from the new so as not to forget your old family?*

Listen to Yourself Caty finds herself falling in love with Snow Hunter and imagining a life with him. But she knows that choosing such a life would forever separate her from her friends and possibly from her family as well. She asks, "Am I brave enough to follow my own still, small voice? Would Mother and Papa still love me?" (page 128) *What do you think Caty should do? Given what you know about how the book ends, how do you think her friends and family would have reacted if she had married Snow Hunter? What do you think you would do in her situation?*

Where Is Home? Even after being returned to her mother and father, Caty writes, "Dear God, will I ever come home?" (page 145) *What does Caty mean by this? What does the word "home" mean to you?*

Standing in the Light After he has read her diary and sees her distress, Caty's father tells her, "Thee learned to open thy heart to those who are different from thee, Caty. That is why thee stood in the light. But such learning is very lonely and cannot be taught to others, for thee had to suffer greatly to uncover such truth." (page 152) He is referring back to something he said to her before her abduction, "If thee stands in the light, Caty, thee will always know the right thing to do. There is a still, small voice in each of us that speaks for God." (page 16) *Do you agree that Caty stood in the light? Why is this a good title for the book? Can you think of another that works better?*

~ACTIVITIES~

Busy Day Ask students to reread page 10, recounting chores and activities done by Caty and her family. Then ask students to make a list of their daily chores and activities. Discuss how it compares to Caty's. Use the comparisons to discuss the many ways our lives have changed in the past 200 years.

Herbs as Medicine Ask students to research how herbs are used as medicine. Divide students into pairs and have them research individual herbs. Ask them to write a report on the herb that includes such information as where the herb is found, ways in which it is used, and how long it has been used. Ask each group to include an illustration of the herb in its report. Then have students share their research with the class.

Nature Calendar Ask students how Caty keeps track of the months and the seasons when she is in captivity (by the changes in nature). Refer them to pages 61, 73, 74, 78, 80, 99, and 121 for examples. Ask students to make a calendar for the coming year. They should illustrate each month with a picture that represents the natural world during that time of year.

Learn About the Lenape Have students research more about the Native Americans who captured Caty and her brother by visiting the Lenni Lenape Historical Society and Museum of Indian Culture Web site at www.lenape.org.

Answers for Attached to the Earth
1. g 2. d 3. h 4. b 5. f 6. c 7. a 8. e 9. answers will vary
10. answers will vary

Attached to the Earth

After writing a list of items that she and the Lenape make from nature, Caty says, "We are attached to the earth by a thousand threads." (page 114)

Below are eight items that Caty makes, as well as the objects that she uses to create them. Draw a line from each end product to the natural object from which it is made.

What Caty makes	**What she makes it from**
1. brooms	**a.** the juice of wild crabapple
2. water dippers	**b.** clay
3. bowls	**c.** turtle shells
4. pots	**d.** gourds
5. chisels	**e.** sumac and black walnut bark
6. rattles	**f.** beaver teeth
7. red paint	**g.** bird feathers
8. black paint	**h.** the wood of the sassafras tree

Now think of ways you are attached to the earth. Think of one object you use that is made from nature. Write about it. Then brainstorm at least one more useful object that you can create using something from the natural world. (For example, you could use a rock to make a paperweight.)

9. One object I use that is made from nature is _____

_____

_____

_____

_____

10. One object that I could create from nature is _____

_____

_____

_____

_____

Colonial America

Tying It All Together

✳ DISCUSSION ✳

Religious Beliefs Compare Mem's and Caty's religious beliefs. How were they alike? How were they different? How important was religion in both their lives? How important is religion in your own life?

Meeting Native Americans Compare Mem's and Caty's experiences with Native Americans. How did each character feel about these people before meeting them? What experiences did each have with Native Americans? How did each character feel about these people by the end of the book?

Ordinary Heroes Do you think ordinary people can be heroes? How are Mem and Caty heroes? Do you know any ordinary people who are heroes? Who are they? Do you think you are or ever will be a hero? Explain.

A Hard Row to Hoe How difficult were Mem's and Caty's lives? How hard did these girls have to work? Which one do you think worked harder? Why?

Trading Places Imagine you could go back in time and trade places with Mem or Caty. Which character would you trade places with? Why?

Choosing Friends If you could be friends with Mem or Caty, which character would you choose? Why?

Life During Colonial Times Based on your reading of these two books, what was life like for most people during colonial times? What were their main concerns? What were their main activities? Would you like to have lived during that time period? Why or why not?

✳ ACTIVITIES ✳

Mem and Caty Meet Ask students to forget about time constraints and to imagine that Mem and Caty meet and tell each other their life stories. Then ask students to write a diary entry for each girl, giving her impression of the other girl's life.

Book Reviews Ask students to write a review comparing the books *A Journey to the New World* and *Standing in the Light*.

Lessons Learned Ask students to write down three things they learned from each book. Combine these and make a class list to see how much students learned from their reading.

Family Ties Family was very important to Mem and Caty. Ask students to imagine that each character has to finish the sentence, "My family is important to me because . . ." Ask students to finish the sentence for each character. Then ask them to finish the sentence for themselves. Ask, how do the three answers compare?

1764 British Parliament passes the Sugar Act, placing tariffs on sugar, coffee, wine, and other products imported into America, to help pay off debt for the Seven Years War. Many colonists protest: "No taxation without representation." The Currency Act prohibits the colonies from printing their own paper money.

Parliament passes both the Quartering Act, requiring that colonists provide food and shelter for British troops, and the Stamp Act, setting tariffs on many kinds of printed matter such as newspapers, legal documents, and playing cards. The Stamp Act is repealed the next year, following a colonial boycott of British goods.

1767 Parliament passes the Townshend Acts, imposing import duties on glass, lead, paints, and tea sent to the colonies. Boston and other major ports boycott British goods. Britain sends in troops to enforce the Acts.

1770 In March, British troops clash with colonists over the quartering of 400 British troops in and around Boston, opening fire on a rock-throwing mob, killing five—the Boston Massacre. In April, Parliament repeals all the Townshend duties, except the tax on tea.

1773 The Virginia House of Burgesses appoints Patrick Henry, Richard Henry Lee, Thomas Jefferson, and others to the newly formed Committee for Intercolonial Correspondence. This committee serves as a network of citizens whose aim is to inform colonists of relevant events.

Parliament passes the Tea Act to save the British East India Company from bankruptcy, thereby giving them a virtual monopoly on tea shipments to America. In December, colonists dressed as Native Americans dump 342 chests of British tea into Boston Harbor.

1774 After the Boston Tea Party, Parliament passes the Coercive Acts (called "Intolerable Acts" by the colonists), closing the port of Boston until colonists pay for the destroyed tea; put-

ting the royal governor in charge of all civil officials; and requiring the quartering of British soldiers anywhere in Massachusetts, even in private homes. Troops are sent to Boston to enforce these acts.

The First Continental Congress meets in Philadelphia (September–October).

1775 British troops head to Concord to destroy American military supplies. Paul Revere and William Dawes ride during the night of April 18–19 to alert the colonists that the British are coming. At dawn, British soldiers meet the Minutemen at Lexington. The first shot of the war is fired.

In June, the Second Continental Congress raises an army and appoints George Washington as military commander. The British sustain heavy losses in the Battle of Bunker Hill.

1776 On July 4, members of the Continental Congress sign the Declaration of Independence in Philadelphia.

Later that year, Washington loses the battles of Long Island, White Plains, and Fort Lee. The British chase the Continental Army through New Jersey, until Washington's troops cross the Delaware River into Pennsylvania. In December, Washington's troops go back across the Delaware to rout the British at Trenton and Princeton.

1777 While British troops occupy Philadelphia, Washington establishes a winter camp 20 miles away at Valley Forge.

1779 Captain John Paul Jones captures the British warship *Serapis* off the coast of England in the most famous naval battle of the war.

1781 On October 17, British General Cornwallis surrenders at Yorktown.

1783 In September, John Adams, Benjamin Franklin, and John Jay represent the United States at the signing of the Treaty of Paris, formally ending the war. Congress ratifies the treaty the following January.

The Journal of William Thomas Emerson

A Revolutionary War Patriot

♦ Summary ♦ The Journal of William Thomas Emerson, a Revolutionary War Patriot by Barry Denenberg gives readers a look at what life was like in Boston from the summer of 1774 through the spring of 1775, through the eyes of a twelve-year-old boy. The boy, Will, is an orphan who runs away to Boston. There he finds work, home, friends, and something to believe in at the Seven Stars Tavern. Through Will's eyes, readers can see how harsh life was in pre-Revolutionary War Boston and better appreciate the sacrifices every person had to make in America's quest for liberty. They can also see how all of us can play an important role in shaping the world around us, no matter our age.

♦ Prior Knowledge ♦ Ask students what they know about events leading up to the American Revolution. What was life in the colonies like in the years preceding the Revolution? What important events took place in and around Boston, Massachusetts, at that time?

～ GLOSSARY ～

agitation: nervousness and worry

alternative: one of two or more things to be chosen

anarchy: a situation without order or control

apothecary: pharmacist

apprentice: someone who learns a craft or trade by working with a skilled person

ardent: with strong feeling

atone: to make up for something

bank: to cover a fire with fresh fuel

bankrupt: totally lacking a particular thing

baubles: small ornaments such as jewels and rings

bellows: an instrument whose sides are squeezed to pump air into something such as an organ or a fire

benevolent: kind and helpful

blaspheme: to fail to show respect and love for something considered sacred

blockade: the closing off of an area to keep people or supplies from going in or out

boarder: a person who pays to live somewhere and receive meals

boisterous: wild and noisy

boorish: rude, insensitive to others' feelings

bound out: placed under the custody of someone

brutish: rough and violent

burly: strong and with large muscles

burrow: to tunnel

cease: to stop

coax: to persuade someone gently to do something

combative: eager to fight

commodity: something useful or valuable

confidential: secret

contempt: total lack of respect

countenance: expression, look

dear: highly valued

delude: to mislead

demented: mad, insane

desert: to run away from the army

diminish: to become less

discharge: to relieve of a charge, load, or burden

distemper: an often deadly disease

dunning: persistently demanding payment

eaves: the part of a roof that hangs over the side of a building

emit: to release or send out

faction: a group marked by its disagreement with others

fanatic: someone who is wildly enthusiastic about a

belief, cause, or interest

feeble: very weak

fife: a small musical instrument similar to a flute

firearm: a weapon that shoots bullets

flint: a very hard, gray stone that creates sparks when struck against steel

folly: foolishness

forsake: to give up, leave, or abandon

fracas: a noisy fight

garrison: a group of soldiers stationed in a town

gout: a disease marked by painfully swollen joints

grievous: serious

gruff: rough or rude

handbill: a printed sheet to be distributed by hand

hazardous: dangerous

hostile: unfriendly or angry

hypocrite: someone who pretends to have virtues, beliefs, or principles that he or she does not actually possess

idle: not busy, not working

inclination: natural disposition

indolent: lazy

ink horn: a small portable bottle for holding ink

insolent: insulting and outspoken

inventory: a complete list of items that one owns

jostle: to bump or push roughly

lamentable: regrettable

lobsterbacks: the name given British soldiers because of their red coats

loyalists: colonists who remained loyal to the British crown

lurk: to lie hidden

meagerness: lack of quality and quantity

melancholy: very sad

musket: a gun with a long barrel

mute: silent, or unable to speak

nefarious: evil

oppression: unjust or cruel exercise of power

patron: customer

perilous: dangerous

pillory: a wooden device with holes for securing the head and hands, once used to punish people publicly

powder horn: a flask for carrying gunpowder

precaution: something one does in order to prevent

a dangerous or unpleasant event from happening

precisely: exactly

proposal: suggested plan or idea

protractor: a semicircular instrument used for measuring and drawing angles

provisions: supplies

quadrant: an instrument used for measuring altitudes

quill box: a pen box

reconciliation: the act of becoming friendly after a disagreement or fight

refrain: to stop oneself from doing something

remedy: something that relieves pain, cures a disease, or corrects a disorder

resolve: determination

retaliation: revenge

sentry: guard

sinister: evil and threatening

sober: serious or solemn

steadfast: firm and steady, not changing

stye: a red, painful swelling on the eyelid

submission: the act of yielding oneself to the power or authority of another

suffice: to be enough or adequate

survey: to measure an area in order to make a map or plan

tallow: fat from cattle and sheep that is used to make candles or soap

tankard: a tall, one-handled drinking vessel

tedious: tiring and boring

tolerate: to put up with or endure

toll: if something takes its toll, it results in serious damage or suffering

tranquillity: the state of being calm and peaceful

treason: the crime of betraying one's country

trespasses: sins

trifle: to play with or not take seriously

turmoil: great confusion

tyranny: cruel and unjust rule

utmost: the most, or greatest possible

varnished: glossed

viper: a type of poisonous snake

virtuous: morally good

whitewashing: whitening with a mixture of lime and water

wields: uses a weapon or tool effectively

∼ DISCUSSION QUESTIONS ∼

A Mere Country Boy? When Will meets Henry Moody he writes, "You could see that he still thought he was superior—talking to a mere country boy." (page 13) *Why do you think people from the city can be prejudiced against people from the country and vice versa? Have you ever been caught up in such prejudices? Explain. After Henry is bitten by a snake, Will writes, "Henry no longer treats me like a simple country boy and we are good and true friends." What made Henry change his opinion of Will? What does this say about the prejudices people hold?*

Public Punishment When he is first in Boston, Will sees the pillory and whipping post being used. (page 22) *What do you think of the pillory and the whipping post as forms of punishment? What would you do if you saw someone you knew in a pillory or at a whipping post? How would you feel if it were you in the pillory or the whipping post? Do you think we should use similar punishments today? Why or why not?*

Loyalists or Innocent Victims? The Fitch sisters argue that if they don't have British goods to sell they will find themselves poor in no time. But Mrs. Thompson and others say they are wrong to sell British goods. (page 26) *What do you think? Are the Fitch sisters right or wrong to sell British goods? If you were in their shoes and read Mr. Wilson's article in the newspaper (page 30), what would you do?*

Tarred and Feathered Will writes about Mr. Carlisle, long suspected of being loyal to the crown, finally getting "what he deserved" when his house is burned to the ground and he is tarred and feathered. (page 26) *Do you think patriots were right to treat suspected loyalists this way? Why or why not?*

Boys and Babies Mrs. Thompson admires the job Will is doing with Becca, saying that "You usually can't count on boys to be good with babies." (page 43) *Do you agree with Mrs. Thompson? Why or why not?*

Trust Carries a Dear Price When Mr. Wilson gives Will his first assignment, he asks him not to tell anyone, not even Henry or Mrs. Thompson. "At times like these, trust carries a dear price and you must err on the side of caution," Mr. Wilson says. "The less said the better." (page 64) *Do you agree with Mr. Wilson? If you were Will, would you have been able to keep the secret, especially from your best friend? What events in the book go on to prove the wisdom of Mr. Wilson's words?*

To Die For When Will asks a British soldier whom he is helping to desert, "Why are you doing this?" the soldier tells Will, "The real truth is that the most important decision a man can make in his whole life is what he is willing to die for." (pages 67–68) *Do you agree? Why or why not? If so, what, if anything, are you willing to die for? If not, what do you think is the most important decision a person can make?*

Scared to Be Afraid? Will writes, "Sometimes I just like to be scared. To see if I can take it. I don't like to be afraid of anything." (page 77) *How do you feel? Do you like to be scared? Do you mind being afraid of things? What, if anything, do you think being scared says about you as a person?*

Quartering Act Will writes, "If having British soldiers camping right in the middle of town wasn't enough, they are now being put up in people's homes." (page 92) *Do you think the Quartering Act, in which colonists were required to provide British soldiers with food and housing, was* *fair? Why or why not? Imagine that the U.S. government asked you to let American soldiers live in your home. How do you think you and your family would react? What would you do?*

An Eye for an Eye After the death of Henry Moody, Mr. Wilson writes, "Blood has been shed and for it blood must atone." (page 115) *Do you agree? Why or why not?*

Americans One and All In an article Mr. Wilson writes, "Virginians, New Englanders, Pennsylvanians, Marylanders. No, I say. Americans. Americans one and all." (page 117) *Why do you think Mr. Wilson wrote that? How important do you think it was for the colonists to have a common name?*

Staying Put At the end of the story Will writes, "I have decided to stay here with Mrs. Thompson." (page 130) *Why do you think Will wanted to stay? What would you have done had you been in his shoes?*

~ ACTIVITIES ~

Two Sides to Every Story Write two letters to the imaginary editor of a colonial Boston newspaper about the Quartering Act: one from a patriot and one from a loyalist. Discuss how and why the opinions of these people differ. Is either "side" entirely right or wrong? Explain.

Coded Letter Ask students to write a letter with a hidden message like the one on page 83. They can use the same device as the author of that letter did, by making every fifth word the one that counts, or they can think up their own code. Then ask students to exchange letters and decipher them to find their real messages. Students who chose different codes for their letters should give their readers a hint as to what their code is. (In the book, the code was "five.")

What's in a Name? The name of one of the British warships in Boston harbor is the *Viper*, which is the name of a venomous snake. Ask students whether or not they think this is a good name for a warship. Then have students imagine that they are going to christen a brand new warship and ask them to brainstorm a list of names for their vessel. Ask each student to choose one name and then draw or paint a picture of his or her warship, with its name clearly emblazoned on the side.

It's About Time Divide students into small groups. Ask each group to research the major events leading up to the American Revolution and present them on a time line. Have students share their time lines with the rest of the class and encourage them to add any important events that they may have missed.

Chores! Ask students to look at the list of Will's chores on page 18. Then ask them to list all the chores they do around the house. How do the lists differ? Why do they think children today have fewer chores than boys and girls in the 18th century?

Answers for Get to the Point

Answers will vary, but article can easily be cut in half without losing meaning. Bonus: a loyalist.

Get to the Point

Mr. Wilson is a man of few words. When Will relates his life story the man tells him, "Get to the point, get to the point." And when Will asks him for advice on becoming a good writer, Mr. Wilson answers, "Never use two words when one will do." Use Mr. Wilson's advice to edit the following article. Rewrite your version on the lines below.

An Unloyal Attack on a Loyal Subject

Just yesterday Boston's esteemed Mr. Joshua Carlisle suffered most horribly at the hands of unruly people called patriots from the town of Boston when they attacked his honorable person and grand home. The crowd absolutely destroyed his grounds before setting fire to and burning down his lovely house. Most thankfully Mr. Carlisle was not in the burning house. But he suffered immeasurable damage to his pride when he was covered with sticky, gooey hot tar and then rolled in the feathers from the inside of his slit-open feather bed. Most thankfully again, Mr. Carlisle suffered no serious bodily harm or damage. The authorities have not yet arrested even one person for this horrible injustice because the criminals managed to disguise themselves exceedingly well.

_____

_____

_____

_____

_____

_____

_____

_____

_____

Bonus: Do you think the author of this article was a loyalist or patriot?

_____

The Winter of Red Snow

The Revolutionary War Diary of Abigail Jane Stewart

◆ *Summary* ◆ *The Winter of Red Snow: The Revolutionary War Diary of Abigail Jane Stewart* by Kristiana Gregory tells the story of the Continental Army's 1777–1778 winter at Valley Forge, Pennsylvania, through the eyes of an eleven-year-old girl. The winter shows Abby the harsh realities of war, from bloody footprints in the snow to the brutal hanging of a deserter. It also allows her to discover her own strength, and that of those around her, when she is faced with 12,000 American soldiers camped in her front yard and enemy troops stationed just 18 miles away. This winter also teaches Abby to value who she is and the life she lives. When the soldiers leave Valley Forge at the end of the winter, Abby writes, "I shall remember our soldiers. I shall remember to complain not about being cold or having unpleasant chores."

◆ *Prior Knowledge* ◆ Discuss life during wartime. Ask students what it might be like for civilians as well as for soldiers. Ask students what, if anything, they have ever heard about Valley Forge, Pennsylvania. Do they know the role this town played in the American Revolution? Also, discuss the book's title, *The Winter of Red Snow*. Ask students to brainstorm possible meanings of this title.

∼ GLOSSARY ∼

aide-de-camp: a military aide

alliance: a friendly agreement to work together

ally: a person or country that gives support to another

amputate: to cut off someone's leg, arm, finger, etc.

apprentice: someone who learns a trade or craft by working with a skilled person

arrogant: conceited, too proud

artillery: large, powerful guns that are mounted on wheels or tracks; the part of the army that uses large guns

Baptist: a member of a Protestant denomination

bayonet: a long knife that can be fastened to the end of a gun barrel

brigade: a unit of an army

butter churn: a machine or device in which milk is made into butter

carcass: the body of a dead animal

chamber pot: a portable container kept in the bedroom used for going to the bathroom

chaplain: a priest, minister, or rabbi who works in the military, a school, or a prison

civilian: someone who is not a member of the armed forces

cloak: a loose coat with no sleeves that is wrapped around the shoulders and fastened at the neck

cobbler: someone who makes or repairs shoes

console: to cheer up or comfort

court-martial: a trial by military officers

devotee: an eager follower or supporter

devotions: an act of prayer or private worship

drill: to teach someone how to do something by strict training, discipline, or repetition

encampment: the place where a group, such as a body of troops, sets up camp

fife: a small musical instrument similar to a flute

grate: a grid of metal bars in the base of a furnace or fireplace

handbill: a small printed sheet to be distributed by hand

hearth: the area in front of a fireplace

heartsore: heartsick, depressed

hide: the skin or pelt of a large animal used to make leather

inkwell: a container for ink

inoculation: an injection of a weakened form of a disease into someone's body in order to treat or prevent that disease

knickers: loose, short pants that end just below the knee

larder: a small room or pantry in which food is stored

lavish: to give in great amounts

linger: to stay or wait around

looking glass: a mirror

lye: a strong substance, made by soaking wood ashes in water, that is used in making soap

mayhaps: maybe, perhaps

minuet: a slow, graceful dance

musket: a gun with a long barrel that was used before the rifle was invented

naught: nothing

notion: an idea

parchment: heavy, paperlike material, made from the skin of sheep or goats, that is used as a surface on which to write

penknife: a small knife with blades that fold into a case

provisions: supplies

pullet: a young hen

pulpit: a raised, enclosed platform in a church where a minister stands to address a congregation

pumps: shoes

quarter: to provide people, usually soldiers, with food and lodging

queue: a braid of hair

quickstep: a spirited march tune; a lively step used in marching

quill: the long, hollow central part of a bird's feather used to make a pen

rafters: the parallel beams that support a roof

ranks: lines of soldiers standing side by side

resolution: a formal expression of opinion made by an official body

roasting spit: a long, pointed rod that holds meat over a fire for cooking

root cellar: a cellar usually covered with dirt, used to store root crops and other vegetables

serenade: a vocal or instrumental performance in honor of someone

shilling: a coin once used as money

shorn: cut or clipped

skirmish: a minor fight in a war

spectacles: eyeglasses

starch: a substance used for making cloth stiff

stout: large and heavily built

strudel: a pastry made from a thick sheet of dough, rolled up with filling, and baked

sutler: a civilian shopkeeper who maintains a store on an army post

tan: to convert an animal hide into leather by soaking it in a solution containing tanning-rich bark

taproom: barroom

tin whistle: a small, metal wind instrument

toddy: a usually hot drink made up of liquor, water, sugar, and spices

trellis: a crisscross framework of thin strips of wood used to support growing plants

tricorn: a hat with three corners

trill: a vibrating, high-pitched sound

tripe: the stomach lining of an ox or cow

trundle: a low bed that can be slid under a higher bed when not in use

waistcoat: a short, sleeveless coat or vest

wickets: a game played by using mallets to knock wooden balls through small wire arches called "wickets"

wretched: miserable

~ DISCUSSION QUESTIONS ~

An Army in Your Front Yard Although Abby isn't quite sure what to think of the situation, her mother and father are worried when they learn that General Washington and his troops are going to march to Valley Forge to make winter quarters. As a neighbor explains, it will mean "*thousands of soldiers in our front yard for the whole winter . . . .*" (page 9) *Why do you think Abby's parents were upset when they learned where Washington's troops would spend the winter? How would you feel if you learned that thousands of soldiers were going to camp in your front yard for the winter?*

Bloody Footprints Abby watches the soldiers as they arrive in Valley Forge. She writes, "The men were quiet and thin. The sight of them took my breath away . . . . Their footprints left blood in the snow." (page 12) *Discuss what this description tells you about the state of Washington's army. Does the title* The Winter of Red Snow *mean something different to you now?*

Feast and Famine As Abby helps to prepare food for Christmas dinner she remembers the soldiers and wonders, "Were we bad to have so much food when they have so little?" (page 18) *What do you think? Was it wrong for Abby's family to have so much food when the soldiers had so little? Why or why not? What, if anything, do you think Abby and her family could have done differently at Christmas? Have you ever felt as Abby did, guilty that you had so much compared to others? If so, what, if anything, did you do about it?*

To Share or Not to Share Abby's father brings grain to the soldiers and makes shoes for them. But not all families will share what they have with the soldiers. (page 22) *Do you think everyone should share with the soldiers? Why or*

why not? What about people, such as the Quakers, who do not believe in war? What would you do if you were in the Stewart family's shoes?*

School to Hospital When she returns to school on January 2, Abby writes, "We walked the cold mile to school, but were turned away because it is now a hospital!" (page 26) *Do you think the army had a right to take over the school and turn it into a hospital? Why or why not?*

Harsh Punishment for Deserters After Abby and her family see the body of a man who was hanged for deserting the army, Abby writes, "A terrible day . . . . I hate the army." (page 28) *Why do you think the punishment for desertion was so severe? Do you think it was too severe? Why do you think soldiers tried to desert despite the threat of death?*

Business Is Business, or Is It? Abby's aunt sells bread to the British commander, and Abby wonders, "How could she!" (page 40) She writes about her Philadelphia relatives, "none felt ashamed about accepting gold coin from the enemy. 'Business is business,' mine uncle said to Papa." (page 44) *What do you think? Is it wrong to sell to the enemy? Or, as Abby's uncle said, is it all right because, "business is business"? What would you do if you were in Abby's aunt and uncle's position?*

A Coat Fit for a Dog Elizabeth secretly cut up her blue cloak to make a coat for the handsome Frenchman, Pierre. Her mother later told her, "No matter how good thy deed may be, if thou art dishonest along the way that good deed will always be tainted." (page 78) *Do you agree with Mrs. Stewart's words? How did they end up coming true in this story?*

A Secret Burden When Lucy runs away she writes to Abby telling her, "Tell not a soul" of her whereabouts. (page 104) Abby is torn, however, because she cannot stand to see Lucy's parents so sick with worry. Abby writes, "What am I to do? If I tell, Lucy shall feel betrayed, but if I keep her secret . . . . Is it proper to let her family suffer so?" (page 111) *What would you do if you were in Abby's shoes? What do you think of what Abby finally did? Have you ever been in a position similar to Abby's, where you did not want to betray a friend by revealing his or her secret, but felt that someone was being hurt by your withholding information? If so, what did you do? Were you glad you did that?*

No One Is Perfect At the beginning of the story, Abby is jealous of Elizabeth, saying her sister is much prettier than she. But by the end she writes, "Odd, but I am no longer jealous of Elizabeth. She is much prettier than I, but she is not perfect." (page 128) *Why do you think Abby is no longer jealous of Elizabeth? Have you ever been jealous of someone and then got over that feeling when you learned more about that person's life? Explain.*

It Could Always Be Worse When the soldiers leave, Abby writes, "I shall remember our soldiers. I shall remember to complain not about being cold or having unpleasant chores." (page 138) *Why does Abby write this? Have any events or situations in your life ever left you saying the same sort of thing? Explain.*

The Glory of War Nearly 2,500 soldiers died that winter at Valley Forge and there was not even a battle. *Some people say that war is a glorious thing. What do you think? Did your view of war change as you read this book? Explain.*

~ ACTIVITIES ~

Infant Mortality Before the birth of Abby's brother John, Abby had five brothers who died in infancy. Abby writes, "We have not had a brother live through his first winter." Ask students why so many babies did not survive their first year in the late 18th century. Have them research to find the answers. Then ask students to make a chart showing the rate of infant mortality from Abby's time to the present. Discuss how and why it has changed over the years.

Bounty The word *bounty* is defined as "something that is given generously." During the Revolutionary War, many people made Bounty Shirts and Bounty Coats for soldiers in need. Ask students to brainstorm about those in need in your community. If winter is coming, there may be a shortage of gloves and mittens, or perhaps there is a soup kitchen that could use more canned goods. Have students identify a particular need and then make a plan to meet it. For example, for a glove/mitten drive, students might send notices home to all families in the school, asking for donations of a pair of mittens or gloves from whoever can afford to give. Students can then arrange for a place for the mittens to be dropped off, sort them by size, and make plans for their distribution.

Writing Letters Mrs. Hewes tells Abby that General Washington writes 15 letters a day, mostly to Congress, pleading for food, clothing, and other supplies. Ask students what concerns they have that can and should be addressed by elected officials. Then ask each child to write a letter to a local representative about that concern.

Charles Willson Peale Abby and Elizabeth saw Charles Willson Peale sketching a portrait of George Washington. Divide students into small groups and ask them each to find a portrait of George Washington (in a biography, an encyclopedia, etc.) and to research the artist who painted it. Students may also wish to try copying the portrait. When they are finished, have them share their reports with the rest of the class.

Extra! Extra! Ask students to research France's formal recognition of the United States and its agreement to send aid in February 1778. Then invite them to write an article that might have appeared in an American newspaper at the time, describing the relationship between the two countries and what it means to the new United States.

Answers for Speaking of the Revolution
1. liberty 2. taxation 3. colonies 4. hang (twice) 5. life
6. fight 7. try 8. equal Bonus: Declaration of Independence

```
L F I G H T D E
I C L A R A A T
F I O N O X F I
E N E Q U A L D
L I B E R T Y E
C O L O N I E S
T R Y P E O N D
E N C H A N G E
```

Speaking of the Revolution

The American Revolution was fought with words as well as weapons. Here are some famous quotes from that time in U.S. history. Each quote is missing a word (except for number 4, which is missing the same word twice). Find and circle the missing words in the word-search box. Then write the words on the lines where they belong.

fight	colonies	taxation	hang
life	liberty	try	equal

1. "I know not what course others may take, but as for me, give me __ __ __ __ __ __ __ or give me death." Patrick Henry (1736–1799)

2. "No __ __ __ __ __ __ __ __ without representation." James Otis (1725–1783)

3. "The die is now cast. The __ __ __ __ __ __ __ __ must either submit or triumph." King George III (1738–1820)

4. "We must indeed all __ __ __ __ together or, most assuredly, we shall all __ __ __ __ separately." Benjamin Franklin (1706–1790)

5. "I only regret that I have but one __ __ __ __ to give for my country." Nathan Hale (1755–1776)

6. "I have not yet begun to __ __ __ __ __." James Paul Jones (1747–1792)

7. "These are the times that __ __ __ men's souls." Thomas Paine (1737–1809)

8. "We hold these truths to be sacred and undeniable; that all men are created __ __ __ __ __." Thomas Jefferson (1743–1826)

```
L F I G H T D E
I C L A R A A T
F I O N O X F I
E N E Q U A L D
L I B E R T Y E
C O L O N I E S
T R Y P E O N D
E N C H A N G E
```

Bonus: In 1776, Richard Henry Lee, one of Virginia's delegates to the Continental Congress, presented a resolution that resulted in the creation of what document? Write the letters that aren't circled in the word box (left to right, top to bottom) to find the answer.

The __

Revolutionary War

Tying It All Together

✴ DISCUSSION ✴

All About War Imagine Will and Abby meeting after the winter of 1777. What do you think each of them could tell the other about war that she or he doesn't already know?

Liberty Isn't Easy How did Will and Abby suffer by supporting the cause of liberty? Is it just soldiers that suffer during wartime? Explain.

Growing Up Fast In what ways were Will and Abby forced to grow up before their time? Explain.

Trading Places If you could go back in time and trade places with Will or Abby, which would you choose? Why?

Help the Enemy? Imagine a British soldier was wounded and came looking for help. How would Will respond to this request? How about Abby?

Deserters Compare and contrast British and American deserters. Why did the soldiers desert? How were they punished? What do you think of these punishments?

✴ ACTIVITIES ✴

Map It Out Ask students to draw a map showing the most important places mentioned in *The Journal of William Thomas Emerson: A Revolutionary War Patriot* and *The Winter of Red Snow: The Revolutionary War Diary of Abigail Jane Stewart*. Such a map should show Massachusetts and Pennsylvania, with Boston, Concord, Lexington, Valley Forge, and Philadelphia among the places identified. Have students calculate the approximate distance between where Will and Abby lived.

Citizen at Valley Forge Ask students to imagine that Mr. Wilson visited Washington's troops at Valley Forge. Then have them write an article trying to use Mr. Wilson's voice to describe what he found there.

Desert Ask students to reread the handbill encouraging British soldiers to desert, on page 48 of *The Journal of William Thomas Emerson*. Then ask each student to create two handbills—one trying to encourage British soldiers to desert, the other trying to encourage American soldiers to desert.

1763 The British issue a proclamation forbidding settlement west of the Appalachian Mountains and reserving the area for Native Americans.

1769 Daniel Boone begins to explore land west of the Appalachian Mountains.

1787 Congress passes the Northwest Ordinance, so that "the utmost good faith shall always be observed towards the Indians; their lands and property shall never be taken from them without their consent."

1803 The United States signs the Louisiana Purchase with France, nearly doubling in size with the $15 million purchase of an 828,000 square-mile parcel of land (the largest single land acquisition the United States will ever make).

1803- Meriwether Lewis and William Clark explore
1806 the Louisiana Purchase territory to find "the most direct and practical water communication across the continent for purposes of commerce."

1820 The Missouri Compromise permits Missouri to enter the Union as a slave state and Maine as a free state (temporarily maintaining the balance between slave and free states), and forbids slavery in the Louisiana Purchase north of 36° 30' latitude.

1820s The government begins to move Native American groups into Indian Country, the land west of the Mississippi.

1821 Opening of the Santa Fe Trail, an important caravan route from Independence, Missouri, to Santa Fe.

1825 Opening of the Erie Canal, allowing boats to travel from the Great Lakes to the Hudson River and on to the Atlantic Ocean.

1830 The Indian Removal Act calls for the removal of all Native Americans from land east of the Mississippi.

1836 Texas declares its independence from Mexico and becomes a state in 1845.

1838- American soldiers forcibly remove 16,000
1839 Cherokees from their Georgia home and march them 1,200 miles to a reservation in Oklahoma. About 4,000 die during this "Trail of Tears."

1842- John C. Frémont, guided by Christopher "Kit"
1844 Carson, maps the Oregon and California trails; thousands of settlers travel west.

1845 Journalist John L. O'Sullivan coins the term Manifest Destiny, which provides a rationale for settling the entire continent.

1848 Gold is discovered at Sutter's Mill, California, creating a gold rush that lasts until the start of the Civil War.

After the Mexican War ends, the United States wins more than 500,000 square miles of Mexican territory, including what is now California, Nevada, Utah, and Arizona, and parts of New Mexico, Wyoming, and Colorado.

1862 Congress passes the Homestead Act, which grants 160 acres of public land to anyone over 21 years old. More than two million people will claim land and build new lives out West.

1864 The Long Walk (actually several walks) forces Navajos to move more than 300 miles through winter snows from their homeland in north-eastern Arizona and northwestern New Mexico.

1869 The transcontinental railroad is completed. Until this time, more than 300,000 people traveled west by wagon train along the California and Oregon trails.

1871 The Indian Appropriations Act terminates the treaty process between Native Americans and the federal government, stating that tribal affairs can be handled by the federal government without tribal consent.

1890 The massacre of more than 200 Native Americans at Wounded Knee ends centuries of warfare between Native Americans and settlers.

1898 Congress passes the Curtis Act, which overrides previous treaties promising Native Americans that their lands will never be included in any state or territory without their approval.

Across the Wide and Lonesome Prairie

The Oregon Trail Diary of Hattie Campbell

◆ *Summary* ◆ *Across the Wide and Lonesome Prairie: The Oregon Trail Diary of Hattie Campbell* by Kristiana Gregory tells the story of a thirteen-year-old girl's journey from Booneville, Missouri, across the Oregon trail into Oregon City, Oregon. Hattie experiences sorrow and joy in equal measure during her seven-month journey. She mourns the deaths of fellow travelers and friends, while celebrating new life and new beginnings. Hattie grows during her journey. Early on she is quick to judge people by appearances or by what others say about them. But she eventually learns that it is what is inside a person that makes her good or bad.

Thus she is able to befriend the 300-pound Mrs. Bigg and to look at Native Americans as fellow humans rather than as enemies. Hattie's journey is a grueling one, but through it she grows to be better, stronger, and braver—all qualities that help her start her new life.

◆ *Prior Knowledge* ◆ Ask students if they know what the Oregon Trail was. Where did it start? Where did it end? Ask students why people left their homes and headed to an unknown land. What was the journey like? What hardships did pioneers suffer? Was it worth making the journey?

~ GLOSSARY ~

altitude: the height of something above ground

ambush: to hide and then attack someone

associate: to keep company with

axle: a rod in the center of the wheel around which the wheel turns

barometric pressure: the pressure exerted by Earth's atmosphere

barter: to trade by exchanging food and other goods or services, rather than by using money

berth: a bed in a ship, train, or airplane

bluff: a high steep bank or cliff

brow: the edge of a steep place

calico: plain cotton cloth printed with a colorful pattern

camisole: a short, sleeveless undergarment for women

chafed: raw and sore from rubbing

churning: moving roughly

confide: to tell someone a secret

corral: a fenced in area for horses, cattle, or other animals

current: the movement of water in a river or ocean

doily: a small piece of lace or cut paper placed under a plate or other item, used as decoration or to protect furniture

emigrant: someone who leaves their own home to settle in another place

enterprising: having a lot of good ideas or enough bravery to undertake new and challenging projects

epidemic: an infectious disease that spreads quickly from person to person

ford: to walk across the shallow part of a stream or river

grove: a group of trees growing or planted near one another

gruesome: disgusting and horrible

homestead: to settle a tract of land under the Homestead Act

hospitable: generous and friendly to guests, making them feel at home

keel: to fall over and faint

low: to utter the deep low sound characteristic of cattle; to moo

petticoat: a thin, skirt-like garment worn underneath a skirt or dress, often with ruffles, meant to hang down below the hem of outer garments

polygamist: someone who has more than one spouse at a time

prairie schooner: covered wagon

preserves: jam

provisions: supplies

pulpit: a raised, enclosed platform in a church where a minister stands to address a congregation

rapids: a part of a river where the water flows swiftly

ravine: a deep, narrow valley with steep sides

recollect: to remember

rump: the back part of an animal, above its hind legs

Sabbath: the day of rest and worship in some religions

sagebrush: a shrub that grows on the dry plains of the western United States

sandbar: a ridge of sand formed in a river or sea by the action of tides or currents

satchel: a bag or small suitcase sometimes carried over the shoulder

serenade: a vocal or instrumental performance in honor of someone

shivaree: a noisy mock serenade, usually given for a newly married couple

solemn: very serious

sorcerer: a person who performs magic by controlling evil spirits; a wizard

splint: a piece of wood, plastic, or metal used to support an injured limb

stake: to support with a piece of wood or other material that is pointed at one end

tarp: a heavy, waterproof covering, usually made of canvas

tea cozy: a padded cover for a teapot to keep it warm

theology: the study of religion and religious beliefs

tinker: a person who travels from place to place mending pots, pans, and other metal utensils

torrent: a violent, swiftly flowing stream of water

wheelwright: a person who makes or repairs wheels and wheeled vehicles

~ DISCUSSION QUESTIONS ~

A Shocking Announcement Hattie describes her father's announcement that they are going to head west as "shocking." (page 5) *How would you feel if your parents announced that you were going to pack up and leave everything behind to move to a new place in just one month?*

Manifest Destiny President Polk said it was Americans' "Manifest Destiny," to spread democracy all the way to the Pacific coast. (page 8) This theory, coined by newspaper editor John L. O'Sullivan in 1845, said that Americans had a God-given right, even a duty, to take over any land they desired. *Do you agree with O'Sullivan's theory of Manifest Destiny? Why or why not? Who do you think benefited from the widespread support of this theory? Who do you think suffered?*

Donner Disaster Hattie writes about the Reed and Donner families, who were stuck in the mountains during the winter and resorted to cannibalism to survive. She writes, "No one says much about them, but I often think about the terrible, terrible business of eating dead friends. I'm brave, but not near brave enough to do that." (page 23) *What would you do to survive? Do you think you would resort to eating dead people? Hattie writes that it took a kind of bravery to do that. What do you think?*

Are Appearances Deceiving? Hattie writes of Mrs. Kenker, "How can someone who looks like my dear old grandmother be a thief?" (page 40) *Have you ever been deceived by a person's appearance? Explain. Why do you think people judge others by their appearance? Is it a good or bad thing to do?*

Who's to Blame? Cassia and several other children died from eating the hemlock that Hattie and Pepper thought was wild parsnip. Afterwards Hattie writes, "Everyone says I'm not to blame, but still I feel dead inside." (page 46) *Do you think Hattie or anyone else is to blame for*

the children's deaths? Is there always someone to blame when there is a tragedy? Why or why not? Why do people look for someone to blame?*

Keeping Rules When discussing Brigham Young, Hattie's father says, "Don't judge a man only by how strict he keeps rules." (page 58) *What does Hattie's father mean by this? Do you think how strict a person keeps the rules is the only way to judge a person's character? Explain.*

"Indians are like white folks" After several non-violent encounters with Native Americans, Hattie writes, "I have decided Indians are like white folks in that some are honest and kind, others are liars and thieves." (page 105) *Do you think Hattie's thoughts about Native Americans could apply to all people who are of different race, ethnicity, or religious beliefs? Why or why not?*

Mercy When Hattie is especially angry at Mrs. Kenker, Mrs. Bigg tells her, "Hattie, as hard as it is, we need to be kind to Mrs. Kenker, whether she deserves it or not. That's what mercy is, honey." (page 112) *Do you agree with Mrs. Bigg that Hattie should be kind to Mrs. Kenker, whether she deserves it or not? Why or why not?*

"One bite at a time" Hattie's journey is filled with tragedy. Hattie asks Wade why no one ever talks about all the terrible things that have happened. He answers her with a joke: "How does an ant eat a buffalo? . . . One bite at a time . . . ." (pages 118–119) *What does Wade mean by this joke? Do you think it is good advice? Why or why not?*

Come on Out After they have reached Oregon City, Hattie and others write to friends in Booneville telling them to come to Oregon. (page 134) *Why do Hattie and others encourage their friends to make such an arduous journey? If you received such a letter, would you be inclined to go?*

~ ACTIVITIES ~

Exploring Explorers Several explorers are mentioned in this book, including Lanford W. Hastings, John C. Frémont, and Kit Carson. Ask each student to choose and research the life of a person who explored the western part of the United States. Then ask them to make an oral presentation in which they share their findings with the class.

Emigrant's Guide Remind students that pioneers were helped on their journey by reading such books as Lanford W. Hastings's *Emigrant's Guide to Oregon and California*. Ask students to imagine that a person is moving to their city, town, or village from another country. Then work as a class to write an emigrant's guide to your community. Students might want to include such topics as places the emigrant needs to know about (school, library); places he or she might want to visit (park, movie theater, mall, pizza parlor, ice cream store); fun events (fairs, parades); important people (mayor, village trustee, principal); the best way to get around (include a map); and local history. You might want to divide students into groups and give each group a topic on which to work. When students have done their research, ask them to compile a book with illustrations. You might want to make copies of this book to give to families with children who move into the area.

What Are You Afraid Of? Tell students to refer back to Hattie's list of what she was afraid of at the start of her journey. (page 9) Then have them look at how Hattie's fears changed during her travels. (page 60) Ask students why

they think Hattie's fears were no longer the same. Then instruct them to make their own list of what frightens them. Collect their work and put it aside. In six months time, ask students to make another list of their fears. Give them back their original list and encourage them to compare the two. Discuss whether they are the same or different, and why they may have changed. (Take extra care to respect students' rights to privacy. Do not reveal something that a child does not wish to share with the class.)

Poisonous Plants Ask students to make a list of poisonous plants. Each student can then choose a plant to research and write a one-page report. The report should include a simple drawing of the plant, its description, a list of places where it is found, details about how it is harmful, and cures (if any) against its poison. You might want to collect these in a "poisonous plants" notebook.

Tall Tales When Hattie and her fellow travelers discover pools of warm, bubbly water, Tall Joe says one of the pools is named Beer Spring because mountain men swear they get drunk after a few sips. When Hattie repeats this to her father, he says that's likely just another tall tale. (page 98) Discuss what a tall tale is and ask each student to write a tall tale about something that happened in his or her life. Share the tall tales with the class.

Answers for Milestones Along the Oregon Trail
Refer to the map on page 161 of *Across the Wide and Lonesome Prairie* to check placement of milestones.
Bonus: About 150 miles

Milestones Along the Oregon Trail

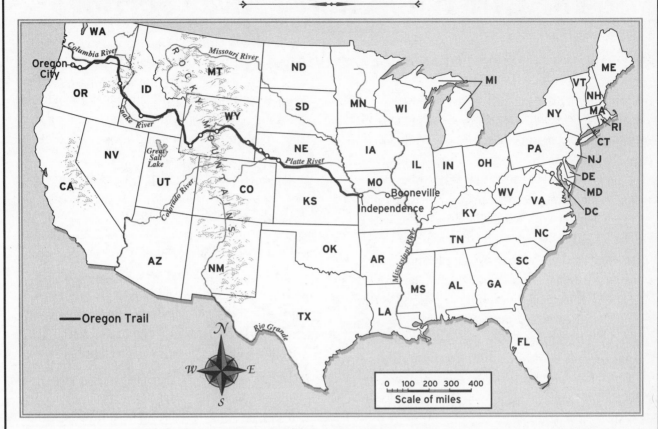

Look at the map of the Oregon Trail. It shows where the trail started and where it ended, but does not identify any of the milestones in between. Use a ruler, the scale of miles, and the information below to fill in the map so that it shows many of the landmarks of Hattie's journey.

Landmark	Mileage from start of trail
Independence	0
Ash Hollow	504
Chimney Rock	561
Scott's Bluff	596
Fort Laramie	650
Independence Rock	815
South Pass	914
Fort Bridger	1,026
Three Island Crossing	1,398
Flagstaff Hill	1,601
Barlow Pass	1,878
Oregon City	1,930

Bonus: Approximately how many miles did Hattie and her family travel to get from Booneville to Independence? _____

The Girl Who Chased Away Sorrow

The Diary of Sarah Nita, a Navajo Girl

◆ *Summary* ◆ *The Girl Who Chased Away Sorrow: The Diary of Sarah Nita, a Navajo Girl* by Ann Turner is the story of the Long Walk as Sarah Nita tells it to her granddaughter many years later. Sarah Nita tells that when she was twelve, American soldiers burned her home and captured her parents while she and her sister watched helplessly from a nearby mesa. Frightened and alone, the two made their way to the *tseyi*, in search of relatives and safety. There they found relatives, but not safety, as the soldiers soon captured most of the Navajos on that land. The soldiers then marched Sarah Nita and her people hundreds of miles through the cold, bitter winter, first to Fort Defiance and then to Fort Sumner, where Sarah Nita and her sister were reunited with their parents. Through this long, difficult period, Sarah Nita managed to keep alive her hopes and those of the people around her by telling stories. That is how she became The Girl Who Chased Away Sorrow.

◆ *Prior Knowledge* ◆ Ask students what they know about the lives of Native Americans in the late 19th century. What was their relationship to the land? What was their relationship with new settlers? Ask students if they know anything about the Navajos. Have they ever heard of the Long Walk? What about the Trail of Tears? Where do many groups of Native Americans live today? How did they get there?

∼ GLOSSARY ∼

brushwood: the wood of small branches that have been cut or broken off

burrow: a tunnel or hole in the ground

card: to clean, untangle, and collect fibers using a card, to prepare for spinning

compound: an area of land, usually fenced in

corral: a fenced area that holds horses, cattle, or other animals

cradle board: a wooden frame worn on the back, used for carrying a baby

flint: a very hard, gray stone that makes sparks when struck against steel

gourd: a hard-shelled fruit with a rounded shape similar to that of a squash or pumpkin

grouse: a small, plump game bird

gully: a long, narrow ravine or ditch

loom: a machine used for weaving cloth

mesa: a hill or mountain with steep sides and a flat top

mica: a mineral that separates into very thin pieces

notched: marked with cuts shaped like a "V"

nurture: to feed and protect

ocher: an earthy, yellow iron ore often used as a pigment

puma: another name for a cougar

raiders: individuals who make sudden, surprise attacks on a person or place

ruff: a collar of feathers or hair on the neck of certain birds or animals

scrabble: to scratch or claw about clumsily or frantically

scuttle: to scurry, or run with short, quick steps

sinew: cord or band of dense, tough tissue that connects a muscle with a bone; a tendon

spindle: a round stick or rod used on a spinning wheel to hold and wind thread

tasseled: adorned with cords or threads at one end

wayside: the side of the way or land next to a road or path

yucca: a plant in the lily family

~ DISCUSSION QUESTIONS ~

Premonitions Before the soldiers come to her home, Sarah Nita says, "I hate this shivery feeling on my neck; it has happened a few times before, and something bad always followed." (page 11) *When else did Sarah Nita have premonitions that something bad was about to happen? Did her fears prove true? Have you ever had feelings like Sarah Nita did, that something bad was about to happen? Did your premonitions prove true or false? How important do you think it is to listen to your feelings? How important was it to Sarah Nita?*

The Girl Who Chased Away Sorrow When Sarah Nita tells her father the story of The Girl Who Chased Away Sorrow, her father tells her, "Your name should be that." (page 16) *Why does Sarah Nita's father say that? Do you agree with him? Why or why not? What effects do Sarah Nita's stories have on herself and others throughout the book? Find an example of Sarah Nita chasing away sorrow by telling a story. Do you think stories can make a person feel better? What are some other ways people chase away sorrow? Do you have a special way? If so, what is it?*

Pretending to Be Brave After the soldiers take away Sarah Nita's family she decides that the only thing she can do is pretend to be brave. (page 35) *Why does Sarah Nita feel she has to pretend to be brave? Do you agree that is something she must do? Who will feel better if Sarah Nita pretends to be brave? Do you think pretending to be brave can actually lead to being brave? Explain your answer. Have you ever pretended to be brave to do something that frightened you? Did pretending help you? Explain.*

Just Punishment? When High Jumper complains bitterly about the encroaching settlers, Grandfather tells him that the Navajo are being punished for raiding their ranches

and taking their sheep and horses. (page 44) *Why do you think the Navajo raided the settlers' land and took their sheep and horses? Were they right or wrong to do so? Were the settlers justified in punishing the Navajo by burning their fields, stealing their sheep, and removing them from their homeland? Why or why not?*

Worrying About the Future When Sarah Nita finds herself starting to worry about how safe the *tseyi* is, she remembers something her mother used to say, "Only a foolish person borrows trouble from the days to come." (page 49) *What did Sarah Nita's mother mean by this statement? Do you agree with her? What is gained by worrying about the future? What is lost?*

Foolish or Brave? After High Jumper shoots an arrow at several settlers, giving away the family's hiding place, Sarah Nita says she thinks that he is both foolish and brave. (page 66) *What do you think? Was High Jumper foolish, brave, or both for shooting an arrow at the settlers when he did? How do you think you would have felt if you were in his shoes? What do you think you would have done? Have you ever done anything that might be called foolish and brave?*

A Friend Among Enemies? When discussing the soldier they call Mica Eyes, Kaibah reminds Sarah Nita of one of their mother's sayings, "even among enemies, there can be a friend." (page 85) *Do you agree that there can be a friend among enemies? Why did Sarah Nita have such a hard time believing that Mica Eyes was their friend? Do you think he was their friend? Why or why not?*

Who Needs to Be Civilized? At one point, the Nakai comes riding up to the captured Navajos and says, "We will civilize you." Grandfather exclaims that it is the settlers who need to be civilized. (page 105) *Do you think it is up to one group of people to civilize another? If so, how should it be decided which group civilizes and which group is civilized? How was it decided in the case of the pioneers who moved west and the Native Americans? Do you think this was right or wrong? Explain. If their positions had been equal, what could the settlers have taught the Navajos? What could the Navajos have taught the settlers?*

Befriending the Enemy   As Kaibah becomes more and more friendly with Mica Eyes, Sarah Nita becomes more bothered by their friendship. *Why was Sarah Nita bothered by her sister's friendship with Mica Eyes? How would you have felt if you were in Sarah Nita's shoes? What if you were in Kaibah's shoes?*

Evil Wishes   Sarah Nita says, "Father always told me I must never wish for evil to come on anyone." Yet she can't help wishing evil on the blue soldiers for what they are doing to her and her people. But these dark thoughts make her feel sick inside. (page 106) *Do you agree or disagree with Sarah Nita's father that you should never wish for evil to come to anyone? Explain your answer. Why did Sarah Nita feel badly after wishing evil on the blue soldiers? What did she do to make herself feel better? Have you ever wished evil on someone? How did it make you feel? What, if anything, do you think is a better way to deal with a negative situation?*

Running Away   Several times High Jumper tells Sarah Nita about men and boys who are talking about running away. (pages 100–101, 116–117) Sarah Nita always worries that High Jumper will go with them. *Why does High Jumper want to run away? Why does he decide against it? What would you do if you were in his shoes? At one point High Jumper does run away. Why? Do you think he did the right thing? Why or why not?*

Desperate Times   Sarah Nita gets corn for her father by picking kernels from horses' dung. (page 163) *There's a saying, "Desperate times require desperate measures." How does this apply to the way in which Sarah Nita finds corn to make her father feel better? Could you imagine doing the same thing? Why or why not?*

～ ACTIVITIES ～

Writing About the Past Ask students to choose a grandparent or elderly friend, relative, or neighbor to interview about an important time in that person's life. Then ask students to write that story, just as Sarah Nita wrote her grandmother's story. Ask, how important is it to learn about the lives of the people who came before us? Is there anything you learned during this project that surprised you or gave you new insight into the person you interviewed?

Giving Names Remind students that Sarah Nita the granddaughter writes, "Grandmother tells me she can remember the journey because she gave names to everything that happened: the Day of Burning, . . . Silver Coat Finds Water . . . ." (page 1) Ask students to look back over the past year and give names to important events in their lives. Discuss how giving a name to something can help you remember it later.

Rugs Tell a Story Ask students what part rugs played in Sarah Nita's story. Then instruct them to research Navajo rugs and rugmaking.

Have students draw designs for their own Navajo-style rug and share their designs with each other. Ask what story, if any, their rugs tell.

Growing Gold Discuss the importance of corn to Sarah Nita and her people. Ask students how important corn is in their lives. Then have students grow their own corn plants as a class project.

Chase Away Sorrow Instruct students to look back over the many stories that Sarah Nita told throughout this book. (See pages 16, 31, 96, 111, and 165.) Discuss the stories' simplicity and the effect they had on Sarah Nita's listeners. Ask students to relate their own stories to the class. They either can make up something for this activity or retell past favorites. Have them make these stories as similar to Sarah Nita's as possible—short, simple, and uplifting.

Answers for Super Similes
1. e 2. h 3. a 4. g 5. c 6. f 7. d 8. b Bonus: answers will vary

Super Similes

Sarah Nita uses lots of similes to tell her story. A *simile* is a way of describing something by comparing it to something else, using the words *like* or *as*. Sarah Nita uses a simile when she says, "our people start moving like a river." Below are other similes Sarah Nita uses, but they are broken apart. Draw a line from the word or words in the first column to the phrase that Sarah Nita uses for her comparison in the second column.

1. white men	**a.** like a clean road
2. corn	**b.** like being in a whirlwind of bad spirits
3. part in hair	**c.** like a sharp smell on the wind
4. long buildings	**d.** like a sharp knife
5. restlessness	**e.** like locusts settling everywhere
6. soldiers' words	**f.** like pebbles hitting a bowl
7. cold water	**g.** like dark, old bones
8. crossing the river	**h.** like gold lying in heaps on the animal skins

Bonus: Try your hand at creating similes. Use your imagination to complete the first three similes and then write three more of your own.

1. The party was so much fun it was like _____

_____

2. If I wore that outfit I would feel like _____

_____

_____

3. Getting a shot at the doctor's is like _____

_____

4. _____

_____

5. _____

_____

6. _____

The Journal of Sean Sullivan

A Transcontinental Railroad Worker

◆ *Summary* ◆ *The Journal of Sean Sullivan: A Transcontinental Railroad Worker* by William Durbin tells the story of a fifteen-year-old boy who leaves his home in Chicago to join his father, a foreman for the Union Pacific, in Omaha. Sean wants very much to be with his father, who seems to be lost in grief since returning from the war and finding himself a widower. Sean also wants to be part of the history-making adventure of building the railroad. He is disappointed when he has to start out at the bottom as a water-carrier, but is later thankful because this work helps him gain the strength to reach his goal of becoming a spiker. Sean gains more than physical strength during the two-and-a-half years he works on the railroad. He also gains the strength to take a stand against the widespread prejudice around him. By the time he takes a maul from a Chinese worker and drives in one of the railroad's last spikes, Sean is a man doing a man's job, building a railroad, making history.

◆ *Prior Knowledge* ◆ Ask students what they know about the transcontinental railroad. What is it? When was it built? Why was it built? Who built it? What was the work like? Who benefited from its construction? Who suffered from its construction?

∼ GLOSSARY ∼

abalone: a large sea snail with a flat shell whose meat is used for food and whose shell lining is a source of mother-of-pearl

alkali: a salt present in the soils of some dry regions

anvil: a heavy iron block on which metal is hammered into desired shapes

bore: to make a hole in something

butte: a large mountain with steep sides and a flat top that stands by itself

cartridge: a metal tub containing a bullet or pellets and the explosive that fires them

comeuppance: a deserved penalty

conference: a meeting to discuss matters of common concern

Continental Divide: a divide separating river systems that flow to opposite sides of a continent

contractor: a person who makes a formal agreement to perform work or provide supplies

cribbage: a card game for two or more players in which each player tries to perform various counting combinations for points

derringer: a short-barreled pocket pistol

editorial: having to do with the preparation of a publication

excursionist: a person who goes on a short pleasure trip

fisticuffs: a fight with the fists

flush: exactly even or level

gorge: a deep valley with steep, rocky sides

gully: a long, narrow ravine or ditch

hack: a writer who exploits his or her creative ability or training for money

hawk: to offer goods for sale by shouting in the street

heft: weight, heaviness

hummock: a small rounded hill

hunker: to squat on one's heels

impale: to pierce with something pointed

impeachment: the process of having formal charges brought against a public official who may have committed a crime while in office

liniment: a liquid or semiliquid that is applied to irritated skin

livery: a stable where horses are taken care of for a fee

longshoreman: someone who loads and unloads ships at a seaport

meander: to take a winding or indirect course

mesa: a hill or mountain with steep sides and a flat top

mogul: a person of rank or power

nag: a horse, especially one that is old or worn-out

ornery: stubborn and mean

passel: a group of indeterminate number

pilings: a structure of piles or heavy beams driven into the ground, often under water

pitch: a yellow or brown, sticky substance that oozes from pine, balsam, and other trees and plants; sap

plume: a long, fluffy feather or something that resembles one

puncheon: a split log or heavy slab with the face smoothed

rile: to annoy or irritate

scalawag: a rascal

shanty: a roughly built hut or cabin usually made of wood

slack: not busy or active

smidgen: a small amount

spawn: to produce a large number of eggs

speculation: an investment in a risky venture

stake: to fasten with one or more sticks that are pointed at one end for driving into the ground

stanch: to stop the flow of a liquid

strumpet: a prostitute

surly: mean, rude, and unfriendly

survey: something that has been measured in order to make a map or plan

tippler: someone who drinks liquor, especially by habit or to excess

tote: to carry or haul something

trestle: a type of bridge; a braced framework of timbers for carrying a road or railroad over a depression

trump: to make up something in order to deceive, as an accusation

vigilante: a member of a voluntary committee that punishes crime when the law appears inadequate

wield: to handle a tool

RAILROAD GLOSSARY

coupling pin: a device that connects train cars

cowcatcher: an inclined frame on the front of a train engine designed to throw obstacles off the track

depot: a railroad or bus station

fishplate: a steel plate used to reinforce a joint, made by fastening parts together end to end without overlapping

grade: to make more level

linkage: an arrangement or system of links

mule skinner: a person who drives a team of horses or mules

roundhouse: a circular building used for storing or repairing locomotives

spiker: a person who drives spikes into railroad ties when laying tracks

switch: pair of moveable rails on which a train car can shift from one track to another

tamper: a person who packs something down with a series of light blows

throttle: a valve regulating the flow of steam to an engine

tie: a heavy piece of timber or iron fastened between the rails of a railroad track

~ DISCUSSION QUESTIONS ~

Turning Against the Native Americans
After seeing a scalped man, Sean writes, "Maybe working on the prairie and seeing what happened to men like Bill Thompson could turn anyone against the Indians." (page 7) *Why do you think Sean's father and so many others despise Native Americans? Do you think it's just because of the scalping, or is there more to it than that? Why are Native Americans attacking the railroad workers in the first place?*

Healing Work? Sean's aunt tells him, "Your Pa needs to find a part of himself that he lost in the war. The West may be the answer." (page 14) *What part of himself did Sean's father lose in the war? Did working on the railroad help him find it? Explain your answer.*

Shovel Versus Pen Sean writes, "Pa used to say that a man could accomplish a heck of a lot more with a shovel than a pen, but Mother wouldn't let him get away with it." (page 14) *Can you accomplish more with a shovel or a pen? When might one tool be more effective than the other?*

Competition Sean writes, "So it's the U.P. versus the C.P., and we're not only fighting for money in the bank but for pride. We aim to prove we're the best." (page 30) *How did the competition between the Union Pacific Railroad and Central Pacific Railroad contribute to the building of the transcontinental railroad? How did it take away from it? What do you think of competition? When is it a good thing? When is it a bad thing? Have you ever been helped or harmed by it? Explain.*

Grass Is Always Greener Sean's brother, John, writes, "You are lucky to be working on the railroad . . . ." (page 32) Yet there are many times Sean wishes he were back home in Chicago. There's an expression, "the grass is always greener on the other side of the street." *What does it mean? How does it apply to Sean and his brother? Have you ever felt that way and then gone on to find out that the grass is no greener, but only looks that way from a distance? Explain.*

Mind Over Matter After General Casement moved a stuck wagon that Sean and two others couldn't budge, Sean asked his father how such a small man could be so strong. His father said it was more a matter of mind than muscle. "When a thing needs to happen, he wills it to be." (page 37) *What does the expression "mind over matter" mean? How does it apply to General Casement? Has it ever applied to you? Explain.*

A Woman Doctor? When Sean's father brings him to Cheyenne to have his cut hand examined, both Sullivans are surprised that the doctor is a woman. (page 49) *What jobs today are rarely filled by women? Why? Do you think this will change? If so, how?*

Life Is Cheap Sean writes that if the Dale Creek Bridge had given out, "I bet they would have used us all for fill and carted in some extra dirt to level things off." (page 70) *Why did Sean say this? Do you agree with him? How much value was placed on human life during the building of the transcontinental railroad? Give examples from the book to support your answer.*

Here First During his stint at clearing out rattlesnakes, Sean writes, "I actually feel a little sorry for the snakes. Like the buffalo, they've had this country to themselves for longer than any of us know. Now just because we've decided to build a railroad, we expect them to clear out of our way." (page 77) *Who or what else besides snakes and buffalo might this statement apply to? Do you share Sean's sympathies? Why or why not?*

Just the Facts? After learning how the advertising agency hired by the Union Pacific brings reporters out in plush railcars, pays all their expenses, and gives them fancy meals just so they'll write glowing reports about the railroad, Sean writes, "If that's true, I wonder if I can believe anything I read in the papers." (page 80) *How much influence do you think people, companies, and government agencies have over what is written about them in the newspaper? Do you believe everything or anything you read in the newspaper? Why or why not?*

Vigilante Justice? When a group of men hired by the Union Pacific stormed the Freeman's office and smashed it up, a bunch of town vigilantes attacked them, killing 25 railroad workers and wounding dozens more. (page 106) *Were the Union Pacific workers right in attacking the Freeman's office? Were the vigilantes right in taking the law into their own hands and opening fire on the attacking men? Is it ever right to take the law into your own hands? If so, why, and when? If not, why not?*

Shoddy Work Throughout the book, Sean's father complains about the shoddy work that is being done on the railroad. "What good is track that can't hold up a train?" (page 122) *Why was the work done on the railroads shoddy? How did this end up costing taxpayers even more money? How did Thomas Clark Durant, one of the Union Pacific's founders, pay for this mistake when it came time for the opening ceremony?*

"Lowest sort of thieves" Sean writes about the railroad owners, "People complain about bank robbers and railroad bandits, but to my mind, the owners of these rail lines are the lowest sort of thieves. They are squeezing every dollar they can from the government . . . . I say it is stealing pure and simple." (page 133) *Why does Sean write this about the owners of the rail lines? Give some examples from the book of how they are "squeezing every dollar" from the government. Do you agree with Sean that this is stealing? Why or why not?*

Planting a Grave After several Chinese workers die in "accidents," Sean writes, "It finally happened. The Chinese decided that they'd had enough, and they planted a grave . . . . The blast killed one Irishman, and injured three others . . . . My question is, why does it take someone dying to knock some sense into our heads?" (page 136) *Do you think the Chinese were right to "plant a grave"? Why or why not? Can you think of anything else they might have done to prevent more deaths of their workers? Do you agree with Sean that it takes someone dying to knock some sense into our heads? Why or why not?*

Changing the West On his train ride back to Chicago, Sean sees a lone buffalo galloping along the crest of a hill. He writes, "Lots of folks say it won't be long before the buffalo are all gone, but I'm hoping they can hang on. Only time will tell." (page 157) *What happened to the buffalo? How else did the building of the transcontinental railroad change the West?*

~ ACTIVITIES ~

Keep a Journal Remind students that Sean wrote, "I've learned firsthand that writing can help a person." (page 12) Ask how writing helped Sean and if it has ever helped them. Then ask students to keep a private journal to record their own thoughts and feelings. Every month or so ask students if their writing is helping any of them in the same way it helped Sean.

Big on Buffalo Divide the class into three groups to research buffalo. Ask the first group to read about the history of buffalo in the United States, from their first sightings here, through westward expansion, to the present. Ask the second group to research the animal, to learn such facts as its size, diet, habitat, and social structure. Ask the third group to learn how Native Americans used buffalo. Tell students that after they have completed their research, they are to write a short (two- to three-page) report describing what they discovered. They should use illustrations, charts, and graphs to support their findings. Have each group share their report with the class. You may even want to share all three reports with other classes.

Railroad Math Ask students to look at page 96, where a newspaper reporter is reciting some of the numbers relevant to the tracklaying operation. Play a game in which students have to calculate such things as how many blows to a rail, how many spikes to a mile, and how many rails in ten miles.

All the News? After vigilantes killed 25 Union Pacific workers, the railroad, in an effort to avoid bad publicity, managed to keep the information out of the newspapers. Sean wrote, "I know if Indians had killed those fellows, every newspaper in this country would be scrambling to print the story with a fat headline." (page 107) Ask students to choose a current event and bring in articles from different newspapers and magazines that covered the incident. Then read the collected clippings as a class and compare the points of view of each source. Ask students how what they've learned will affect how they read, listen to, and watch the news.

Impossible Dream? Tell students that back in 1856, people laughed at Theodore Judah when he suggested that the United States build a railroad from New York to San Francisco. The newspapers even called him "Crazy Judah," and drew cartoons and wrote editorials making fun of him. Ask students to draw cartoons poking fun at Judah's naysayers. You might also suggest that they write an editorial to go along with it.

Answers for Transcontinental Railroad
1. Omaha, Nebraska 2. Sacramento, California
3. Promontory Summit, Utah 4. Nebraska, Wyoming, Utah
5. California, Nevada, Utah 6. 1100 miles 7. 675 miles
8. 1775 miles Bonus: May 10, 1869

Transcontinental Railroad

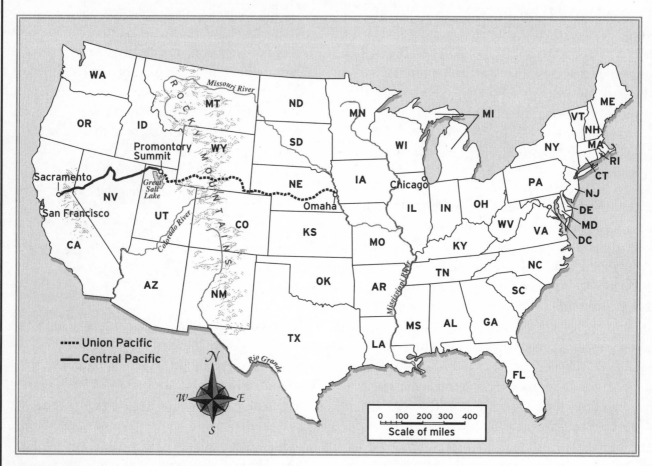

This map shows the transcontinental railroad route and identifies many of the places mentioned in *The Journal of Sean Sullivan.* Look at the map, then answer the questions.

1. Where did the Union Pacific begin laying tracks? _____

2. Where did the Central Pacific begin laying tracks? _____

3. Where did the two railroad companies meet? _____

_____

4. What states did the Union Pacific pass through? _____

_____

_____

5. What states did the Central Pacific pass through? _____

_____

6. About how many miles of track did the Union Pacific include? _____

7. About how many miles of track did the Central Pacific include? _____

8. About how long was the transcontinental railroad? _____

Bonus: When did the two railroads meet?

_____

Westward Expansion

Tying It All Together

Changing Times How did the West change from the time Hattie Campbell began her journey on the Oregon Trail in 1847 to the time Sean Sullivan helped complete the transcontinental railroad in 1869? Were these changes good, bad, or both? Explain.

Bravery In *The Girl Who Chased Away Sorrow*, Sarah Nita says, "They seem to think we have done something brave and astonishing." (page 45) How was she brave? How were Hattie Campbell and Sean Sullivan brave? Which of these characters do you think was the bravest? Give reasons for your answer.

Saddest Thing In his journal, Sean Sullivan wrote, "Dying young has got to be the saddest thing in this whole world." (page 93) What might Hattie Campbell and Sarah Nita say is the saddest thing in the whole world?

Nature What part did nature play in each of these books? How important was it? How was it a help and/or hindrance to each of the characters? Which character valued nature the most? How important is nature to you?

Prejudice Find an example of prejudice in each of these three books. What is the prejudice based on? How does it affect the person or persons who feel it and those it is directed at?

Where Is Home? After watching her mother discard even more of the family's belongings, Hattie asks, "What will be left when we get to Oregon? How will we make a home?" Her mother replies, "Don't worry, Hattie. Our home is our family, not our possessions." (page 109) How do the lives of Hattie, Sarah Nita, and Sean Sullivan support Hattie's mother's statement? What do you think makes a home?

Iron Horse or Iron Snake? Have students write one paragraph reacting to the completion of the transcontinental railroad from the perspective of each of the main characters: Hattie Campbell, Sarah Nita, and Sean Sullivan.

Manifest Destiny Review with students the 19th century belief in the theory of Manifest Destiny—that it was the responsibility of Americans to spread democracy to the Pacific coast, claiming all the land west of the Mississippi in the process. Ask students to draw a historical cartoon showing their support for, or opposition to, this theory.

Two Sides to Every Story Sean Sullivan wrote in his journal after arriving in Omaha, "Maybe working on the prairie and seeing what happened to men like Bill Thompson [who had been scalped] could turn anyone against the Indians." (page 7) Ask students to write a page of dialogue between Sean Sullivan and Sarah Nita that starts with that line.

1860 Abraham Lincoln is elected president, which splits the nation over the issue of slavery.

South Carolina secedes from the Union.

1861 Mississippi, Florida, Alabama, Georgia, Louisiana, Texas, Arkansas, Tennessee, North Carolina, and Virginia join South Carolina to form the Confederate States of America. Jefferson Davis is elected President of the Confederacy.

The Civil War begins on April 12, when Confederate forces fire on Fort Sumter. Declaring a state of insurrection, President Lincoln calls for 75,000 volunteers for three months of military service. He later orders a naval blockade of Southern ports.

In July, at the First Battle of Bull Run (Virginia), outnumbered Confederate forces beat back the Yankees in a crushing defeat. Congress passes an individual income-tax law to raise money to pay for the war. Enlistment periods are increased from three months to two years.

1862 Slavery is abolished in the nation's capital.

In April, 13,000 Union soldiers and 11,000 Confederate soldiers are lost in two days of fighting at the Battle of Shiloh (Tennessee)— more men than America lost in the Revolutionary War, the War of 1812, and the Mexican War combined. In August, at the Second Battle of Bull Run, Confederate soldiers again defeat Union forces.

During the Battle of Antietam (Maryland) in September, General Robert E. Lee takes the offensive but is foiled when a copy of his plans falls into Union hands. Although there is no clear victor, some historians consider this battle a crucial turning point of the war, which until this time had favored the South.

At the Battle of Fredericksburg (Virginia) in December, Lee again manages to rout Union troops despite his opponents' overwhelming numerical advantage.

1863 On January 1, President Lincoln signs the Emancipation Proclamation, which promises freedom to slaves in Confederate states. Two months later, Congress passes the Conscription Act of 1863.

The Battle of Gettysburg (Pennsylvania), July 1–3, is the final turning point of the war. General Lee tries to press into the North but is turned back after three days of intense fighting.

On July 4, General Ulysses S. Grant's long siege of Vicksburg, Mississippi, ends in victory. The Union takes control of the Mississippi River and splits the Confederacy in two.

Lincoln delivers the Gettysburg Address on November 19, dedicating a military cemetery on the battlefield where more than 50,000 soldiers were killed, wounded, or listed as missing.

1864 In January, General William T. Sherman begins his march across the South. His strategy is "total war"—to destroy everything and everyone in his path. In September, he takes Atlanta and sets much of the city on fire. Sherman begins marching to the sea in November, cutting a 40-mile wide path of destruction from Atlanta to Savannah. He reaches Savannah on December 21 and sends Lincoln a telegram offering him the city as a Christmas present.

1865 Lee withdraws from Petersburg in April, ending the six-month siege, and advises President Jefferson Davis to leave Richmond. The entire Confederate government flees the Southern capital, burning it behind them. Surrounded and facing starvation, Lee surrenders to Grant at Appomattox Courthouse (Virginia), signaling the end of the war, in which more than two million Americans were killed or wounded. During his last public address, President Lincoln urges a spirit of generous conciliation during reconstruction.

On April 14, President Lincoln is assassinated at Ford's Theatre by John Wilkes Booth, a Confederate sympathizer.

After fleeing from Richmond, Confederate President Davis is captured in Georgia in May. The last Confederate troops surrender.

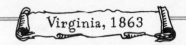

The Journal of James Edmond Pease

A Civil War Union Soldier

◆ *Summary* ◆ *The Journal of James Edmond Pease: A Civil War Union Soldier* by Jim Murphy tells the story of sixteen-year-old James, an orphan who joins the war to have food to eat and a place to sleep. When James joins the Union army, he feels unlucky and not very courageous. But his bravery on and off the field, including his escape through enemy territory back to Union troops, disproves his feelings. By the time he leaves the Army at the age of seventeen, James has risen in rank to second Lieutenant. He has also made friends and found a sweetheart, with whom he will make his own family. His life's journey is epitomized by the words of Sarah, his future bride: "Luck is measured by the friends you make and the people you love." By the end of the story, James is very lucky indeed.

◆ *Prior Knowledge* ◆ Ask students what they know about the Civil War. When was it fought? Why was it fought? Share the Civil War time line with them. Ask students to look at the cover of the book. How old does the main character look? What can they tell about war from the background illustration?

∼ GLOSSARY ∼

adjutant: a staff officer in the armed services who assists the commanding officer

ague: an illness marked by chills, fever, and sweating that recur at regular intervals

array: an orderly arrangement

artillery: large, powerful guns mounted on wheels or tracks; the part of the army that uses such guns

breastwork: temporary fortification

caisson: a chest to hold ammunition

carte-de-viste photograph: a small mounted photograph of a person

cavalry: soldiers who fight on horseback

chevron: a sleeve badge that usually consists of one or more V-shaped stripes that indicate the wearer's rank and service

commence: to begin

consent: approval of what is done or proposed by another

cooper: a person who makes or repairs wooden casks or tubs

courier: messenger

deliverance: rescue

deluge: an overwhelming amount or number

desertion: an act of leaving a military post without permission or intent to return

ford: a shallow part of a stream or river that may be crossed by wading

glower: to look or stare angrily at someone

greenhorn: a newcomer who is unfamiliar with an organization, activity, or area

hardtack: a saltless hard biscuit or bread made of flour and water

laggard: one who stays or falls behind

loafer: someone who is lazy and lacks energy

minié ball: a rifle bullet with a cone-shaped head

mite: a small amount

muster: to assemble in a group

picket: a detached body of soldiers serving to guard an army from surprise

pious: practices religion faithfully and seriously

pontoon bridge: a floating temporary bridge

quinine: a medicine made from the bark of the cinchona tree

recruit: someone who has recently joined an organization such as the armed forces

refugee: a person who runs away to escape danger or persecution

regimental: relating to a military unit called a regiment

reserves: military forces withheld from action for later decisive use

scythe: a tool with a long curving blade fastened at an angle to a long handle that is used for cutting grass or wheat

sharpshooter: someone who is skilled at shooting and hitting a mark or target

siege: persistent attack

silhouette: a two-dimensional representation of the outline of an object

skirmish: a minor fight in a war

sordid: dirty, filthy

stockade: an enclosure or pen made with posts and stakes

sutler: a civilian shopkeeper at an army post

volley: a flight of missiles (such as stones, artillery shells, bullets, and rockets)

∼ DISCUSSION QUESTIONS ∼

Brave or Foolish? Lieutenant Toms tells James he is pretty certain the boy will last to the end of the war because, "You are not one of those crazy patriot fools who sticks his head up high to show how brave you are." (page 4) *What does Lieutenant Toms mean by this remark? Do you think it is a compliment or an insult?*

Eager to Fight? James writes that, to him, guarding the rear of the supply train is as good a job as any, "but does not sit well with the rest of the men, who are eager to see some fighting." (page 6) *If you were in a war, do you think you would feel more like James or more like the other men? Why? Why do you think James is glad of the job that he's got? Why do you think the others want to see some fighting?*

A Terrible Mistake James writes, "What happened at Gettysburg was a mistake. A terrible mistake, but an honest one." (page 11) He adds, "It was what we had been told and taught to do, after all, and no one who was there would have ever blamed us." (page 12)

What happened with James's company at Gettysburg? Can you imagine soldiers making such a mistake? Do you think such a mistake is forgivable? Do you think Lieutenant Toms was responsible for what happened? Do you agree with the people who reduced his rank because of it? What would you have done, if anything, to Company G after the events at Gettysburg?

Leaving Home When James went outside one day to escape the angry stares of his aunt and uncle, he figured he would join his uncle when he came out to work. But his aunt and uncle went about their day never calling or looking for him. After they had clearly gone to bed, James writes, "I started walking down the road, taking away the one burden of theirs that I could." (page 16) *What would you have done if you had been in James's shoes? Would you have stayed even though you were unwelcome or would you have left? What do you think of the way James's aunt and uncle treated him that day? Was it right or wrong? Do you think they had any choice? Explain your answer.*

Substitute Soldiers Henry Clements, a member of James's company, tells James that his family tried to keep him from having to go into the war by buying a substitute. But Henry did not think it an honorable thing to do, so he enlisted. (page 41) *Do you think people should be allowed to buy substitutes to serve for them in a war? Why or why not? Who benefits from such laws? Who suffers? If you were drafted to serve in a war but could buy a substitute to send in your place, what would you do? Why?*

Best Reason to Fight Among James's company, there was some debate about "the best reason to fight in this war." (page 42) *What were some of the reasons the soldiers gave for fighting in the war? What reason do you think was best? Why?*

In the Need of Prayer? One Sunday in December, James stays in his tent writing instead of going to Sunday services. He writes, "I have noticed that in warm weather when we are fighting, many of the men are pious followers, but during the winter when things are quiet and shooting is rare, few respond to the call." (page 47) *Why do you think people are more pious during times of fighting? When else might people be more pious? Explain.*

Learning to Lead When Shelp is giving him a hard time after he is made sergeant, James remembers Sergeant Donoghue's words: "Don't let them get under your hide. If they see they can upset you, they will never let you alone." (page 56) *Do you think this is good advice? Do you think it is easy or difficult to follow? Have you ever been in a situation where your leadership was challenged? How did you handle the challenges? Were you successful?*

Friends When James, Sally, and the others find their way back to Union troops, a private speaks disrespectfully of Sally and the others. James says to him, "These are my friends, Pte., and they saved my life. You will treat them with respect, do you hear?" (page 137) *How did Sally and Davie help James? How did James help them?*

A Change of Heart James is assigned to help unload ambulances until someone can learn the location of G Company. When James learns of its whereabouts, he decides to go find them, even though he doesn't yet have orders to do so. (pages 144) *How did James's goals change over the course of the book? Why did he want to be out fighting instead of helping unload ambulances? Would you have done as he did and left without orders to go back to find your company? Why or why not?*

"People who count on me" At the end of the book James writes, "When I left Uncle and Aunt, I left nothing and headed toward nothing. Now I am heading toward people who count on me and need me, even if just a little. I will probably never be a very brave soldier, but I think I can do my job and do it in an honorable way." (page 146) *What does this statement tell you about the circumstances under which people work best? How important do you think it is to feel needed? If you feel needed, how does it make you feel? If you don't feel needed, how might you change that, as James did?*

"All the luck I will need" James talks about luck throughout the book. Even his last lines, spoken to an officer who has just wished him luck, are: "Thank you, sir. But I believe I have all the luck I will need." (page 147) *How does James's perception of how lucky he is change from the beginning of the book to the end? Why does it change? Do you believe that people are either unlucky or lucky? Why or why not?*

~ACTIVITIES~

Half-Empty or Half-Full? Remind students that when James ended up with a bullet hole in his cap and a minié ball in the journal that he carried under his uniform, Johnny told him, "You are one lucky soldier for sure." (page 36) But James didn't see it that way, believing himself unlucky. Discuss how some people see the glass as half-empty while others see it as half-full. Then ask students to think of something that happened in their lives that could be seen as both positive and negative. Ask them to write several paragraphs describing the experience in a negative light and then several paragraphs describing it in a positive light. Ask, which way of looking at things made you feel better? How might you incorporate this knowledge into your daily life?

Waiting Early on, James writes, "Everybody waits in a war." (page 20) Ask students to think of someone who waits in a war. Ask them to draw a picture of that person waiting and write a small caption underneath. Share the drawings with the class and discuss the many ways that people wait in wartime.

Letters to Soldiers When James receives a letter from Sarah Henderson on Christmas, he says it is the best Christmas he ever had. (pages 49–51) Discuss with students the importance of remembering our country's servicemen and women. You might want to arrange for the class to write letters or make cards to send to servicemen and women during the holidays, or even to a veteran's hospital or nursing home any time.

The Eyes Say It When James looks startled that Sally thought he could help them, Davie tells him, "It was in your eyes, sgt. Sally can tell a lot by the eyes." (page 131) Ask each student to bring in pictures of faces from magazines. Then, as a class, discuss what you think the eyes "say" in each picture. After this discussion, you may wish to have students cut out the pairs of eyes and create a collage.

Civil War Generals Ask students to choose a general mentioned in the book—Union or Confederate—and research and write a short paper about that general. Share these reports with the rest of the class.

Answers for Gettysburg Address
seven, nation, equal, war, great, field, lives; Bonus: Civil

Gettysburg Address

On November 19, 1863, President Abraham Lincoln dedicated a national cemetery on the battlefield at Gettysburg, Pennsylvania. His words have come to be known as one of the greatest public speeches in history. Read the following excerpt from Lincoln's Gettysburg Address. Some of the words are missing. Unscramble each of the words in the word box. Then write the words on the lines where they belong.

"Fourscore and __ __ __ __ __ years ago our fathers brought forth on this continent a new __ __ __ __ __ __, conceived in liberty and dedicated to the proposition that all men are created __ __ __ __ __. Now we are engaged in a great civil __ __ __, testing whether that nation or any nation so conceived and so dedicated can long endure. We are met on a __ __ __ __ __ battlefield of that war. We have come to dedicate a portion of that __ __ __ __ __ as a final resting-place for those who here gave their __ __ __ __ __ that that nation might live."

Word Box

veens _____

aninto _____

quela _____

raw _____

tager _____

delif _____

svile _____

Bonus: What war took more lives than any other war in American history?

The __ __ __ __ __ War.

When Will This Cruel War Be Over?

The Civil War Diary of Emma Simpson

◆ *Summary* ◆ *When Will This Cruel War Be Over: The Civil War Diary of Emma Simpson* by Barry Denenberg tells how the Civil War affected a fifteen-year-old Southern girl. As the Civil War is fought all around her, Emma tries to make sense of what is happening. "Is anything worth dying for?" she asks in her journal. "Is this awful waste—this painful sacrifice—justified in God's eyes?" During the year that she writes, Emma loses her brother to the war and her mother to illness. Her home is occupied and left in a shambles by Yankee troops. While the harsh reality of Emma's life—which mirrors the lives of those around her—makes her old beyond her years, it also teaches her what to value in life. "I fear I have wasted my youth on trivialities . . . . I was living in a state of ignorant bliss. Well, this is no more."

◆ *Prior Knowledge* ◆ Ask students what they know about the Civil War. When was it fought? Why was it fought? Where was it fought? Point out that most of the military activity took place in the South. Ask students to look at the book's background cover illustration. What does it tell them about where and how Emma Simpson lived? Ask, how do you think Emma's life changed when the war was being fought all around her? Have students look at the cover portrait. What does it tell them about the main character?

～ GLOSSARY ～

abide: to tolerate, put up with

Abolitionist: someone who worked to abolish slavery before the Civil War

abomination: something that is horrible or disgusting

acute: sharp or severe

adamant: unshakable

adversity: hardship, misfortune

antidote: something that relieves, prevents, or counteracts

apprehension: suspicion or fear

arduous: very difficult and demanding a lot of effort

artillery: the part of an army that uses large guns

balefully: threateningly

besiege: to surround and attack a place to force it to surrender

blasphemous: the act of saying insulting words about God or a particular religion

blockade: the closing off of an area to keep people or supplies from going in or out

bridle: the straps that fit around a horse's head and mouth that are used to guide or control the animal

casualty: someone who is injured or killed in an accident, disaster, or war

chide: to scold or find fault with someone

chloroform: a heavy, toxic liquid used as an anesthetic

coax: to persuade someone gently and patiently to do something

compassion: a feeling of sympathy and sorrow for someone who is suffering

composure: a state of calm or self-control

conjure: to imagine

consolation: the state of being cheered up or comforted

consternation: a sudden, alarming amazement or dismay that results in utter confusion

contentment: happiness

converse: to talk with someone

conveyance: means of transportation

corporal punishment: physical punishment, such as spanking

counsel: to listen to someone's problems and offer advice

countenance: the look or expression of the face

delude: to mislead

demise: death

deprivation: being without the necessities of life

desert: to run away from the army

desolate: to feel sad and lonely

destitute: lacking food, shelter, and clothing

diligent: working hard and carefully

diminish: to make smaller or weaker

dire: dreadful or urgent

disarm: made to feel friendly or forget your suspicions

disconsolate: cheerless

discourse: conversation

disproportionate: out of proportion

dubious: doubtful

dysentery: a disease characterized by severe diarrhea

emulate: to strive to equal or excel

fickle: of constantly changing opinion

forlorn: sad or lonely

forsake: to give up, leave, or abandon

furlough: a leave of absence granted to a soldier

futile: a waste of time, useless

garret: a room or unfinished part of a house just under the roof

hallowed: sacred or holy

impediment: something that gets in the way

impudent: rude, bold, and outspoken

inconsolable: unable to be cheered up or comforted

indiscretion: wrongdoing

indulgent: letting someone have his or her own way

infernal: hellish

insubordination: disobedience to authority

insurrection: the act of revolting against established authority

intelligence: information; news

lamentable: expressing grief; mournful

loathsome: disgusting

malaria: a serious tropical disease carried by mosquitoes

melancholy: very sad

mirth: gladness that is accompanied by laughter

morphine: a medicine used as a painkiller and sedative

obstinate: stubborn and unwilling to change one's mind

orate: to speak in a showy, pompous way

perseverance: the act of keeping at something; trying and not giving up in spite of difficulties

portico: a porch or walkway with a roof that is supported by columns

proctor: supervisor or monitor

profound: very deeply felt or thought

providence: a God that sustains and guides human destiny

quinine: a medicine made from the bark of the cinchona tree

rapt: fully absorbed

saber: a heavy sword with a curved blade and one cutting edge

shambles: a mess

sharpshooter: someone who is skilled at shooting and hitting a mark or target

soiree: a party held in the evening

solace: comfort, relief from sorrow

staid: sedate, proper, and serious

steadfast: firm and steady; not changing

subjugate: to conquer

superficiality: being superficial, not deep or thorough

supposition: a temporary prediction

tolerate: to put up with; endure

trepidation: fear

typhoid fever: a serious infectious disease with symptoms of high fever and diarrhea that sometimes leads to death

valiant: brave or courageous

vex: to annoy or irritate somebody

wan: pale and sickly

warranted: deserved

waver: to be uncertain or unsteady

wistful: full of unfulfilled longing or desire

woeful: full of sorrow or grief

~ DISCUSSION QUESTIONS ~

New Year's Resolutions At the time she begins her diary, Emma is making her New Year's resolutions. (pages 8–9) *What do you think of Emma's New Year's resolutions? Do you agree that those she made in years past seem childish? What, if any, New Year's resolutions have you made in the past? Have you kept them?*

Escape Into Books Although *Wuthering Heights* is not Emma's favorite book, she writes that she is enjoying it, "for the story takes me far away from my own troubles." (page 16) *Have you ever read to get away from your troubles? What, if anything, do you do to escape your problems? Do you think people need a way to leave their everyday cares and woes behind? Why or why not?*

Don't Know What You've Got Emma writes, "I never realized how happy I was until this war besieged our land." (page 21) *How does the expression, "You don't know what you've got until it's gone," apply to Emma? Have you ever felt that way? Explain.*

Childish Wishes? After receiving a letter from Tally, Emma writes, "I hope it is not childish to think of my own feelings when the war is being waged about such grave issues—but I cannot help that I simply want Tally to return safely." (page 37) *Do you think Emma's wishes are childish? Why or why not? Have you ever, like Emma, felt childish or selfish wishing for something for yourself in the face of bigger concerns? Do you think it is common or rare for people to have such feelings? Explain.*

Father's Beliefs According to Emma's father, "If slavery were as bad as Northerners would have us believe then surely all the negroes in the South would have abandoned the plantations and gone north by now." (page 41) *Do you agree with Emma's father? Why do you think many slaves did not abandon their plantations and go north during the Civil War?*

Beauty and Thorns While walking in her mother's rose garden, Emma remembers, "A rose garden, Mother liked to say, helped remind us that nothing beautiful in life comes without thorns." (page 53) *Do you agree with Emma's mother? Give examples to support your answer.*

Vandals? Emma's father writes "about how important it is to have faith in our just cause and how important it is not to let the Abolitionists subjugate us and take away our country . . . . he will not rest until the vandals are driven from our soil." (page 60) *Why did Emma's father, Colonel Robert Stiles Simpson, believe the Abolitionists were vandals? Do you agree? Why or why not?*

Not All Black and White When "there is talk of negroes leaving," Emma writes that she would be surprised at a slave's "ingratitude" if he left. "We have always treated Nelson as one of our family," she writes. (page 67) *It is clear that Emma supports the Southern way of life, which includes slavery. Does this make Emma a bad person? Why or why not?*

Tables and Chairs After one dinner Emma writes, "It is impossible for me to tell if the negroes understand what is taking place—they come and go as usual, serving dinner while everyone talks as if they were tables and chairs." (page 74) *Do you think the slaves serving dinner understood the war and the dinner conversations taking place about it? What events later in the book show that they did? What does this comment say about how some Southerners treated their slaves? What does it say about Emma's awareness of slaves as people?*

Invading Homes When the Yankees invaded the Broyles's house, a Yankee soldier told Mrs. Broyles that "they were not going to let Rebels sleep comfortably in their homes while their own wounded and sick men suffered." (page 86) *Do you think the Yankees had a right to break into the Broyles's house and steal food, then later take over the house as a hospital? Were they justified in taking over Emma's house? What, if anything, do enemy soldiers owe civilians in a war? Explain your answer.*

Fighting the Same War? After receiving a letter from Tally describing the horrors of war, Emma writes, "I wonder if he and father are fighting the same war." (page 98) *Why does Emma write that? What does her father write about the war? What does Tally write? Why do they view the war so differently? Whose letters do you believe? Why?*

Different Masters Mr. Garlington was murdered by his slaves (page 110), while several of Emma's slaves stayed with her family even after the war was over (page 133). *Why did the slaves treat Mr. Garlington and the Simpsons so differently? How were the slaves treated by their masters? What were some of the similarities in the ways the slaves were treated? What were the differences?*

Is It Worth It? Wondering about her father and Tally, Emma writes, "Is anything worth dying for? Is this awful waste—this painful sacrifice—justified in God's eyes?" (page 129) *How would you answer Emma's questions? How do you think a Union soldier would answer them? How about a Confederate soldier?*

~ACTIVITIES~

Writing for Comfort Have students keep a daily journal over the next month. Ask them to write about what makes them happy as well as what makes them sad. Keep the journals private. At the end of the month, discuss what effect, if any, the writing had on their lives. Did they find, as Emma did, that expressing their "thoughts in writing . . . is a great comfort"? (page 20) Encourage students to continue writing in their journals at home.

Saddest Sight In a letter he writes to Emma, Tally says "a battlefield is the saddest sight he has ever seen." (page 38) Ask students to think of the saddest sight they have ever seen, and then to write a poem about it. If they can't think of something from their own lives, you might want them to write a poem about the battlefield.

Books as Mirrors Initiate a class discussion about the importance of reading in Emma's life. Have students look through the diary to find quotes that Emma copied from books she was reading that reflected experiences from her own life. Then ask students to reread a favorite book and copy at least one passage that speaks to them, that they can learn from or relate to at this time in their lives. Have students share the excerpts they've copied with their classmates and explain the reasons for the selection.

Answers for Civil War Landmarks
1. Fort Sumter 2. Bull Run/Manassas 3. Richmond
4. Antietam 5. Vicksburg 6. Gettysburg 7. Atlanta
8. Appomattox Courthouse Bonus: Gettysburg

Civil War Landmarks

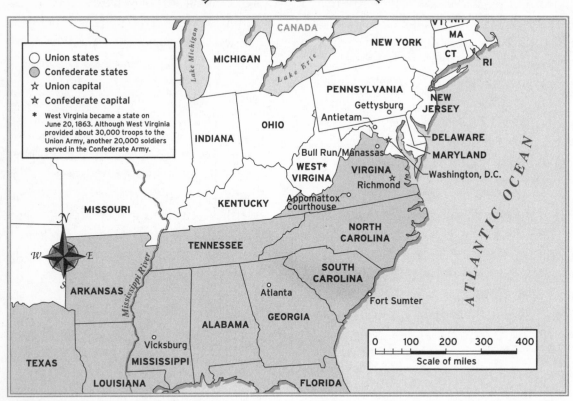

This map shows some of the most important events in the Civil War. Use the map to answer the questions.

1. The Civil War began on April 12, 1861, when Confederate troops opened fire on the Federal garrison at _____, on an island off the South Carolina coast.

2. The first major battle of the Civil War took place on July 21, 1861, at _____, in northern Virginia, just 25 miles from Washington, D.C.

3. The Confederacy chose the central Virginia city of _____ to be its capital in May, 1861.

4. A Confederate retreat after this September, 1862, battle in _____, Maryland, prompted Lincoln to announce the preliminary Emancipation Proclamation.

5. After months of fighting, General Grant's July, 1863, victory in the Siege of _____ proved decisive in winning the Mississippi and the West.

6. The North's July, 1863, victory at _____, Pennsylvania, marked a turning point in the war.

7. In September of 1864, General Sherman seized and burned _____, Georgia.

8. General Lee surrendered to General Grant at _____, in southern Virginia, on April 9, 1865, signaling the end of the Civil War.

Bonus: At which of the places shown on the map did Lincoln make a famous speech?

_____

I Thought My Soul Would Rise and Fly

The Diary of Patsy, a Freed Girl

✦ Summary ✦ *I Thought My Soul Would Rise and Fly: The Diary of Patsy, a Freed Girl* by Joyce Hanson is the story of an orphan slave girl living on a South Carolina plantation right after the end of the Civil War. Patsy, who guesses her age at twelve or thirteen, is much more than she appears. With her lisp and her limp she seems dim-witted and weak, when in fact she is bright and strong. She learns to read by acting the dunce while her young mistress plays school with her. She later uses this skill to help the freed men and women on her plantation learn about what's going on in the world and search for missing relatives in the newspaper. She goes on to teach freed children and adults alike how to read. As she grows in confidence her speech becomes clearer and her limbs become stronger. Patsy never locates her mother or her father but she does find a family in the many people who know and love her.

✦ Prior Knowledge ✦ Ask students what they know about life on a Southern plantation before, during, and after the Civil War. What was it like for the landowners? What was it like for the slaves, and later the freed men and women? Ask students how slaves' lives changed once the Civil War was over?

∼ GLOSSARY ∼

accumulate: to collect things or let them pile up

accustomed: being in the habit or custom

advent: the beginning of something important

ambush: to hide and then attack someone

amnesty: an official promise by a government to release prisoners and pardon crimes

apprentice: someone who learns a trade or craft by working with a skilled person

arbor: a place that is surrounded by trees, shrubs, vines, or other plants

association: an organization, club, or society

bale: to put hay or some other substance into a tightly packed bundle

board: to provide with regular meals and lodging, especially for pay

boil: an infected lump under the skin

boll: the long case that holds the seeds of a cotton plant

bound: placed under legal obligation

calico: plain cotton cloth printed with a colorful pattern

capacity: role, position, or function

cauldron: a large, rounded cooking pot

chain gang: a gang of prisoners chained together as part of a working party

chamber: room

chilblain: a swelling or sore caused by exposure to the cold

chink: a narrow opening

compress: a small cloth pad placed on part of the body to supply moisture, heat, cold, or medication

confinement: the period a mother is confined to bed before, during, and after childbirth

convention: a large gathering of people who have similar interests

curtail: to shorten

degradation: the state of being disgraced and dishonored

elite: a group of people who have special advantages and privileges

emancipation: the act or process of freeing human beings from slavery

fertile: producing vegetation or bearing fruit in great quantities

fortunate: lucky

gin: machine that separates cotton fibers from seeds and waste material

grits: coarsely ground grain, especially corn, boiled and eaten as cereal or as a side dish with meats

homespun: fabric spun or made at home

hominy: hulled kernels of corn

magistrate: a government official who has the power to enforce the law

missionary: a person who is sent by a church or religious group to teach that group's faith and do good works, especially in a foreign country

overseer: supervisor

pallet: a small, hard, or temporary bed

peck: a unit of dry measure equal to eight quarts or one quarter of a bushel

pelt: to strike or beat again and again

pen nib: pen point

penitentiary: a state or federal prison for people found guilty of serious crimes

quarters: lodgings, or rooms where people live

recollection: the act or power of remembering; memory

Regulators: bands of white men who roamed the land to keep the countryside safe from what they called "dangerous blacks"

rickety: old, weak, and likely to break

ringworm: any of several contagious diseases of the skin, hair, or nails caused by fungi and characterized by ring-shaped discolored patches on the skin

row: a noisy fight or quarrel

sharecropping: farming land in exchange for a share of the crop

slate: thin piece of rock or similar material used as a writing surface

swoon: to faint, often from excitement

twaddle: silly or tedious talk

uncouth: rough and rude

vagrancy: the state of being vagrant, or wandering from place to place with no means of support

venerate: to respect greatly

vestige: a trace or sign of something that no longer exists

vigilante: a member of a volunteer group organized to stop and punish crime outside of the law

~ DISCUSSION QUESTIONS ~

Restricting Reading Mistress Davis tells Annie not to play school with Patsy because a visitor might see her and misunderstand. "It is illegal to teach slaves how to read and write," she says. "It spoils them." (page 3) *Why do you think it was illegal to teach slaves to read and write? What would this knowledge do for slaves? How did Patsy learn how to read and write? What did she do with her knowledge?*

Patsy's Problem Patsy writes in her diary, "You see, Friend, I have a problem. When I write to you the words come out easily, not the way I stammer and sputter when I speak, which is why I am so silent most of the time and people think I am dim-witted." (page 8) *Do you think the way a person speaks always reflects how intelligent he or she is? Why or why not? What other examples can you think of in which appearances are deceiving?*

Vagrants? When a Yankee soldier comes to talk to Patsy and others about being free, he tells them, "Anyone found roaming about the countryside without a job or a place to live will be arrested for vagrancy." (page 14) *Imagine you are a former slave. How would you feel if you heard these remarks? Do they help or hinder your sense of freedom?*

"Who did the Yankees free?" Patsy writes, "Somehow I don't think I am free or anybody else is. All of us in The House and in the fields are doing our same tasks. Who did the Yankees free? I wonder." (page 19) *What do you think of when you hear the word "freedom"? What was freedom like for most slaves immediately following the war? Why was the reality so far from the dream? What steps do you think could have been taken to bring the reality and the dream closer together?*

All God's People? Review Father Holmes's catechism to the freed slaves on pages 27 and 28. *What does it say about how many Southerners viewed African Americans? Would you have wanted to go to this church if you were Patsy? Why or why not?*

Keeping Control When the master shouted at the overseer, "Can't you control the hands?" The overseer replied, "If I can't whip them anymore, then I can't control them." (page 30) *Do you think the threat of physical punishment is the only way to get people to listen to you? Explain. Why do you think the overseer at the Davis plantation felt he needed to use physical means to control the farm hands?*

Invisible Girl When Cook describes Patsy right in front of her, it makes Patsy feel badly. "I don't like it when people talk about me as if I am not even in the room." (page 45) *Have you ever had the experience Patsy had, of being talked about as if you weren't even there? How did it make you feel?*

Good Examples After writing about Mister Joe, Patsy writes, "It makes me feel strong to write about brave people . . . . I will try to be like them." (page 63) *Who are some of the people you admire? Why do you admire them? Do you try to be like them?*

A Powerful Tool The Reverend McNeal told the freed men and women at Davis Hall, "All you need is the will and the determination . . . determination . . . is the most powerful tool you have." (page 74) *What do you think of Reverend McNeal's words? Do you think they were helpful to Patsy and the others? Do you agree with them? What do you think was the most powerful tool the freed men and women had? What do you think is the most powerful tool you have?*

Is Politics Important? Patsy writes, "Ruth says that some people think they should not be concerned about politics and voting. They should worry only about schools and land." (page 109) She also writes, "Brother Solomon said that it is not enough to be free. If we have no vote, then we have no power." (page 124) *What do you think? Should the former slaves be concerned with politics and voting or worry only about schools and land? Give reasons for your answer.*

Flying Free By the end of the book, Patsy writes, "I feel like one of those magical Africans who can fly." (page 168) *Why does Patsy feel this way? What has changed since she began writing in her journal? What does the Epilogue tell about Patsy's life? Is it what you would have expected at the beginning of the book? Why or why not?*

~ACTIVITIES~

Black Codes Ask students to research the laws and regulations called the Black Codes and write an essay telling what they were and how they hindered the progress of the freed people.

Take Wing and Fly Ask students to reread the story that Mister Joe tells Patsy about Africans having the magical power to fly. (page 64) Then ask each student to draw an illustration to accompany the story. Share these illustrations with the class.

Phillis Frederick Remind students that Patsy picks the name "Phillis Frederick" for herself after reading *The Third Freedmen's Reader*. (page 162) Ask students to imagine they want to choose a new name for themselves in the same way Patsy did. After they select a name, ask them to write a short essay explaining why they chose it, making sure to include information about the person from whom they derived their name.

Let Freedom Sing You might want to teach your students the song "Free at Last," which is on pages 192 and 193. You can share this song with the rest of the school in celebration during Black History Month.

Answers for Slave Population
1. 700,000 2. 3.3 million 3. 1850 4. 1850, 1860 5. 1.2 million 6. 4 million Bonus: 90 percent

Name _____

Slave Population

This bar graph shows the slave population in the United States from 1790 until 1860. Use the graph to complete the sentences. (Round off answers to the nearest hundred thousand.)

U.S. Slave Population, 1790–1860

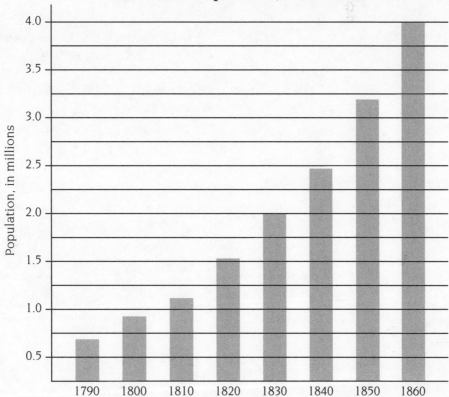

Source: U.S. Department of Commerce, Bureau of the Census

1. In 1790, there were _____ slaves living in the United States.

2. In 1860, there were _____ more slaves than there were in 1790.

3. The slave population more than doubled between 1820 and _____ .

4. The slave population increased by more than 700,000 in _____ and again in _____ .

5. About how many slaves lived in the United States when Abraham Lincoln was born in 1809? _____

6. In 1863, the Emancipation Proclamation freed _____ people from slavery.

Bonus: What was the percentage of slaves living in the United States in 1800 if the total population was slightly more than a million people? _____

The Civil War

Tying It All Together

Aftermath of War For better and for worse, how did the Civil War affect the lives of James Edmond Pease, Emma Simpson, and Patsy?

Friends? Do you think any of the main characters in these three books—James Edmond Pease, Emma Simpson, and Patsy—could ever be friends with one another? Give reasons for your answer.

Common Bonds Despite their many obvious differences, what do the characters of James Edmond Pease, Emma Simpson, and Patsy have in common?

Why Fight? Compare the reasons two or more characters that you read about went to war. Choose from among James Edmond Pease, Robert Stiles Simpson (Emma Simpson's father), Taliaferro "Tally" Mills (Emma Simpson's beloved), and John (Luke's father).

Knowing and Not Knowing In her diary, Emma Simpson writes, "We live with them but we know so little about them." (page 112) Why did most white Southerners know so little about their slaves? And how much did Patsy and the other former slaves at Davis Hall know about their master and mistress? Why do you think the slaves knew so much more about their masters than the other way around?

* ACTIVITIES *

Black Soldiers Remind students that when John came back for Ruth and Luke, Patsy wrote, "I didn't know that there were black Yankee soldiers." (page 126) Ask students to research and write about the role African American soldiers played in the Union Army during the Civil War.

Southern Plantations Invite students to research Southern plantations—cotton or tobacco—before the Civil War. Ask them to find such information as their size, the number of people who lived there, and the kinds of buildings located on site. Then ask students to draw a picture of a Southern plantation along with a brief caption.

Lincoln's Assassination Divide the class into thirds. Tell the first group that for this activity they are to imagine that they are Union soldiers like James Edmond Pease, the second group that they are Southern gentry like Emma Simpson, and the third group that they are freed men and women like Patsy. Then ask each student to write a news story telling of President Lincoln's assassination from that point of view. Compare and contrast the finished articles.

1820s Immigration rises with the end of the Napoleonic Wars in Europe. During this decade, about 150,000 Irish, German, English, and Scandinavian immigrants come to the United States to escape starvation or to find political and religious freedom.

1825 A small group of Scandinavians settle in western New York. Hundreds of thousands will eventually follow and settle in the Midwest and northern plains.

1830s During this decade, 60,000 Europeans immigrate to the United States.

1837 The Native American Association is formed in Washington, D.C. This anti-Irish, anti-Catholic, anti-immigrant organization represents growing feelings of nativism on the part of earlier immigrants, or "native" Protestants.

1840s An Irish potato famine starts a decade in which 1.5 million Irish will immigrate to America. Most settle in seaport cities in the East.

1848 A failed German revolution and a series of crop failures result in a mass immigration of Germans to the United States—one million over the next ten years.

1854 Attracted by the gold rush, 13,000 Chinese immigrate to the United States.

The anti-immigrant and anti-Catholic new American, or "Know-Nothing," Party wins many local races in Massachusetts, New York, and Pennsylvania.

1880 There are 250,000 Jews in the United States. Before 1924, some 2.5 million more will arrive from Eastern Europe and Russia. Many settle in Eastern cities, especially New York.

1882 Congress passes the Chinese Exclusion Act, which bars Chinese laborers from entering the United States for ten years. This act will be extended until it is repealed in 1943.

Congress passes an Immigration Act that bars entry to criminals, paupers, the insane, and other undesirables.

1887 The American Protective Association, an anti-immigrant, anti-Catholic organization, is founded.

1889 Jane Addams opens Hull House in Chicago. This settlement house helps immigrants adjust to life in America.

1892 New York Harbor's Ellis Island opens as an immigration depot; more than 12 million immigrants will pass through it by 1924.

1900s Nearly 9 million immigrants from Italy, Russia, and central Europe pour into the United States during this decade.

1907 Immigration rate peaks as about 1.3 million immigrants enter the United States.

1913 In California the Alien Land Law prevents Japanese from owning land in the state.

1914 Of the 1.2 million persons entering the United States this year, nearly three-quarters are from southern and eastern Europe.

1917 Congress passes a law requiring immigrants to pass a literacy test.

1921 Congress passes the Emergency Quota Act (Dillingham Bill), which establishes a quota system as the basis of immigration policy. Only 3 percent of the total number of people of any nationality (excluding Mexicans and Latin Americans) that already lived in the United States in 1910 may enter each year.

1924 Congress passes the Johnson-Reed Immigration Act, which is even more restrictive than the Emergency Quota Act. The quota of newcomers is now reduced to 2 percent of the total number of people of any nationality that resided in the United States in 1890.

Lowell, Massachusetts, 1847

So Far From Home

The Diary of Mary Driscoll, an Irish Mill Girl

◆ *Summary* ◆ *So Far From Home: The Diary of Mary Driscoll, an Irish Mill Girl* by Barry Denenberg tells the story of how the Great Famine forced fourteen-year-old Mary Driscoll to leave her mother and father in Ireland and follow her sister and aunt to America. Through her journal, we learn of Mary's long, rough voyage across the Atlantic, and of friends made and lost on that voyage. We learn what life in 19th century America was like for poor Irish immigrants—where they could work, where they could live, and how they were treated. When Mary goes to work at the textile mill, the reader, along with Mary, finds backbreaking work, terrible working conditions, and cruel supervisors. Through it all the reader discovers that Mary is a strong and brave girl, one who is willing to risk all she has to help those she loves.

◆ *Prior Knowledge* ◆ Ask students what they know about life in Ireland in the mid-19th century. Why did so many Irish immigrate to the United States at this time? What do they know of the Great Famine? What was the boat ride to America like? What was it like when the Irish got here? Were they welcomed? Where did they live? What did they do for work?

∼ GLOSSARY ∼

afflicted: troubled

bandbox: a cylinder-shaped box used for holding clothing

bask: to lie in or be exposed to a pleasant warmth

berth: a bed in a ship, train, or airplane

bobbin: a spool inside a sewing machine or on a loom that holds thread

boiler: a tank that heats water for a house or other building

bore: to make a hole in something

bowl: the rounded, cup-like, hollow part of a tobacco pipe

card: a machine for cleaning, untangling, and collecting fibers prior to spinning

chamber pot: a container kept in the bedroom and used for going to the bathroom

clan: a large group of families who claim descent from a common ancestor

constable: a police officer

convent: a building where nuns live and work

daft: silly or foolish

deplorable: very bad

depot: a bus or railroad station

doff: to remove or take off

dropsy: an abnormal condition in which a watery fluid collects in certain tissues or cavities of the body, often causing swelling

evict: to force out someone from his or her own home, building, or land

extraction: ancestry, origin

famine: an extreme lack of food

fare: to get along; succeed

flint: a very hard, gray stone that makes sparks when struck against steel

fortunate: lucky

gale: a very strong wind

grave: very serious

labor: a political party that represents the interests of workers

loom: a machine used for weaving cloth

mast: a tall pole rising from the deck of a boat or ship and supporting its sails

melee: a confused struggle

naught: nothing

overseer: supervisor

passage: a journey by ship or airplane

perish: to die or be destroyed

petition: a letter signed by many people asking those in power to change their policy or telling them how the signers feel about a particular issue or situation

premium: a sum over and above the regular price, given as an incentive

privy: toilet

quarantine: the state of being kept away from others to stop a disease from spreading

rogue: a dishonest person

row: a noisy fight or quarrel

salvation: the act of saving or protecting from harm, risk, or loss

scorn: to treat with hatred or contempt

shantytown: a section of a town made up of crudely built huts or cabins

shuttle: the part of a loom that carries thread from side to side

snare: to win or attain by artful or skillful maneuvers

spare: to show mercy or to keep from hurting someone

spire: a structure that comes to a point at the top, often found on church steeples

strife: a bitter conflict between enemies

tavern: a bar

turnout: the number of people at a gathering or event

venture capital: money available to invest in a new enterprise

whitewash: to paint walls and wood fences white using a mixture of lime and water

~ DISCUSSION QUESTIONS ~

The Real America Aunt Nora described America to Mary as, "a sacred place where everyone dresses in red, the color of magic, and the roads are paved with gold." (page 5) *How did Aunt Nora's description compare to what Mary found life in America to be like?*

Closing and Opening The night before Mary is to sail to America, her mother tells her, "Remember, the Blessed Lord would never close one gate without opening another." (page 17) *What does Mary's mother mean by this? Do you agree with her?*

So Far From Home After she has been at sea more than a month, Mary writes, "'Tis a long voyage, and I feel so far from home." (page 37) *What was the voyage like? Could you imagine taking a voyage like this one, alone? Why do you think Mary did? Why did so many others? Did they have a choice? Explain your answers.*

Troubles Not Over The week before they reached Boston Harbor, Sean told Mary his uncle warned him that "your troubles are not over once you've reached harbor. If the authorities think you are ill, they will place you in quarantine or worse, send you back to Ireland."

(page 43) *Describe what happened to Mary and her fellow passengers when they reached Boston Harbor. Do you think the authorities were right to treat immigrants in this way? Why or why not? What do you think you would have done if a member of your family was sent back to Ireland?*

Curiosity and Fear When Mary wakes up early at the Abbotts' house, she finds herself standing at the door leading to Mrs. Abbott's bedchamber. "My curiosity was greater than my fear," she wrote. "I went in." (page 63) *Would you have gone into Mrs. Abbott's room? What might have happened to Mary if she had gotten caught in there? Have you ever been in a situation where your curiosity was greater than your fear? What happened?*

Irish Versus Yankee Girls Kate tells Mary that Mr. Abbott is eager to replace the Yankee girls with as many Irish girls as he can, "because the Irish won't complain about things the way the Yankee girls do." (page 66) *Why do you think the Irish girls won't complain as much as the Yankee girls? How do you think this bodes for the relationship between Irish and Yankee girls in the mills?*

Less Time to Write Compare the frequency and length of Mary's journal entries before and after she starts working at the mill. *How do they differ? Why?*

Only Yankee Girls Annie would like to work in the dressing room but no Irish girls work there. Only Yankee girls. (page 95) *Why do you think Irish girls aren't allowed to work in the dress-ing room? What other forms of prejudice does Annie encounter in America?*

Caged Birds When talking to Annie about working in the mills, Mary is surprised that everyone isn't happy there. "They are always chirping away like little birds," she says. "Even the caged bird sings," Annie replies. (page 108) *What does Annie mean by, "Even the caged bird sings"?*

All Eyes When describing Mr. Fowler, Mary writes, "He's all eyes and no sight, that one." (page 109) *How can someone be all eyes and no sight? Explain. Do you know anyone like that?*

Food and Hope When Sean writes Mary to say that it was a mistake to come to America, that America is not the way he thought it would be, Mary writes, "'Tisn't the way I thought 'twould be, either, but better than back home. At least here there is food to eat and hope for tomorrow." (page 121) *Imagine you are a 19th-century Irish immigrant. Do you think you would be more likely to agree with Sean or Mary? Explain your answer.*

Saving Sean When Mary learned that Sean was in trouble, she left her mill job and took her money to go help him. Annie advised her against it, but, Mary wrote, "I cannot see with anyone's eyes but my own. I must go to Boston. I must take the money I put aside for Ma and Da and bring it to Sean." (page 139) *What kind of friend is Mary? What would you have done if you had been in her shoes?*

~ ACTIVITIES ~

The Great Famine Ask students to research and write an essay on the Great Famine. In particular, they should discuss what caused the famine, how it affected Ireland's population, and what effect it had on immigration to America.

Turning Away the Hungry Discuss what it must have been like for Mary's mother to turn away a hungry woman and her children. (page 14) Then ask students to use the author's description and their own imaginations to try to illustrate this sorrowful scene.

Rough Passage Discuss Mary's voyage to America. Then ask students to choose one of the ship's other passengers and write a series of journal entries telling about the voyage from that person's point of view. (You might want to tell students that, although many of the ship's passengers could not read or write, they can imagine for the sake of this exercise that they all could.) Have students share their journal entries with the class.

Songs for the Heart Ask students to find places in the book where songs helped alleviate sadness. (See pages 21, 29, 57, and 131.) Discuss how songs can cheer people up and ask if and how music has helped them. Then ask students to write their own song verses, using the lullabies that Mary's mother sang as a model.

Character Sketches Divide the class into small groups. Assign each one a character from *So Far From Home* (Mary, Aunt Nora, Sean, Kate, Annie, Laura, Clarissa, Mr. Fowler). Have each group reread how the author has described that person. Then ask students to imagine being that character and write a one-page autobiography. Instruct random students to read their papers aloud, without revealing the characters' names. Then ask the class to guess whom the words describe.

"God save the poor" Have students turn to page 134 where Mary is sick from all her hard work and Aunt Nora is comforting her. "God save the poor," Aunt Nora says. Ask students to brainstorm ways in which they can help those in need, and encourage them to choose a course of action and see it through.

Answers for Immigrants by Country
1. 235,000 2. Ireland 3. 229,000 4. 6,000 5. about 10 percent Bonus: 212,000 (actual figure: 221,000)

Immigrants by Country

This pie chart breaks down immigration to the United States in 1847 by country of origin. Look at the chart, then answer the questions.

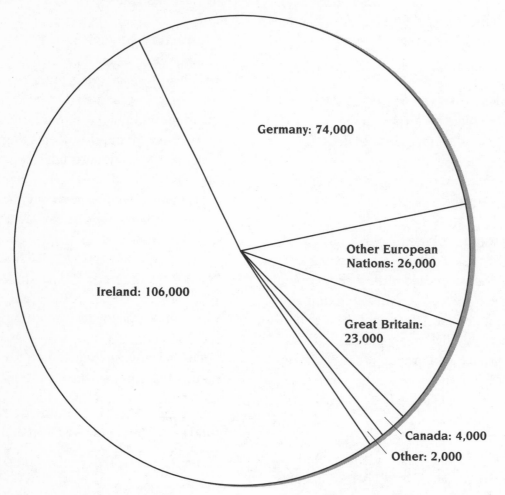

1. How many immigrants came to the United States in 1847? _____

2. What country sent the greatest number of immigrants to the United States in 1847?

_____

3. How many immigrants came to the United States from Europe in 1847?

_____

4. In 1847, how many immigrants came to the United States from countries outside of Europe? _____

5. About what percent of immigrants coming to the United States in 1847 were from Great Britain? _____

Bonus: Irish immigration to the United States peaked in 1851, when it was more than double what it had been in 1847. At least how many Irish immigrated to the United States in 1851? _____

Dreams in the Golden Country

The Diary of Zipporah Feldman, a Jewish Immigrant Girl

♦ *Summary* ♦ *Dreams in the Golden Country: The Diary of Zipporah Feldman, a Jewish Immigrant Girl* by Kathryn Lasky is the story of a Russian Jewish family's immigration to the United States, told by its youngest member, twelve-year-old Zippy. The girl's diary entries take the reader through Ellis Island to New York's Lower East Side with its crowded tenements and harsh working conditions. We learn why the Feldmans left Russia and why, despite everything, America is a better place for them to live. Through Zippy's eyes we see the conflict between the old and the new as Zippy's mother and father clash over the loss of traditions from the old country, and deal with a major family crisis when one of their daughters marries out of their faith. We see them suffer losses but most of all we see them keep hope. Zippy sums this up when she writes, "I want to go on."

♦ *Prior Knowledge* ♦ Ask students what they know about Jewish life in 19th-century Russia. Have they heard of Czar Nicholas, pogroms, or the Russian Revolution? Ask students what they know about the immigrants' passage through Ellis Island, and what life in New York was like for them once they got to the United States. In addition, ask students what they know about Judaism, especially the religion's traditions.

∼ GLOSSARY ∼

acknowledge: to show that you have seen or recognized someone or something

assimilate: to make similar; to conform with the customs of a group

baste: to sew something with loose stitches to hold in place temporarily

bedlam: a scene of uproar and confusion

bias cut: cut on a line diagonal to the grain of the fabric

bobbin: a spool inside a sewing machine or on a loom that holds thread

boudoir: a woman's dressing room, bedroom, or private sitting room

cadence: rhythmic flow of a sequence of sounds or words

carp: a large fresh water fish that is used as food

cloak: a loose coat with no sleeves that is wrapped around the shoulders and fastened at the neck

Cossack: a member of a group of frontiersmen in the southern part of Russia, organized as cavalry in the czarist army

curlew: a large brown bird

elevated: the name given to a subway that is raised above the ground, as over streets

emancipation: freedom from slavery or control

ensemble: the entire outfit, or costume, of an individual

exploit: to treat someone unfairly, usually by not paying enough for his or her work

goiter: an enlargement of the thyroid gland visible as a swelling of the front of the neck

greenhorn: a newcomer who is unfamiliar with an organization, activity, or area

kosher: a word used to describe food that has

been prepared according to the laws of the Jewish religion

kugel: a baked pudding (of potatoes, noodles, bread, or cabbage) served as a side dish or dessert

lame: having an injured leg so as to walk with difficulty

liable: likely or apt

liberal: generous

oppress: to treat in a cruel, unjust way

phenomenal: amazing or astonishing

pinnacle: the highest point of development or achievement

pious: practices his or her religion in a devoted manner

pogrom: an organized massacre of helpless peoples

pushcart: a cart pushed by hand, as one used by street vendors

ruble: the main unit of money in Russia

ruffian: a rough or violent person

sanctuary: a natural area where birds or animals are protected from hunters

scythe: a tool with a large, curved blade fastened at an angle to a handle, used for cutting grass or crops by hand

shirtwaist: a tailored blouse or shirt worn by women

sidelock: a lock of hair worn near or in front of the ear by some Jews

socialist: someone who believes in an economic system in which the production of goods is controlled mainly by government instead of by individual business owners and farmers

spire: a structure that comes to a point at the top

steerage: the part of a ship occupied by passengers paying the lowest rate

streetcar: an electric-powered vehicle that holds many passengers and runs on rails through city streets

swell: a person of high social position

Talmud: the collection of Jewish civil and religious laws

tenement: a run-down apartment building, especially one that is crowded and in a poor part of the city

treadle: a device pressed by the foot to operate a machine

tsar/czar: an emperor of Russia before the revolution of 1917

tsarina/czarina: an empress of Russia, or wife of a tsar, before 1917

understudy: one who is prepared to act another's part or take over another's duties

vile: evil or immoral

Yiddish: the language of European Jews and their descendants, usually written in Hebrew letters

YIDDISH TERMS

bar mitzvah: the ceremony recognizing that a thirteen-year-old Jewish boy has successfully completed a course of study in Judaism

bubeleh: a term of endearment that literally means little doll

bulbe malakh: a term of endearment meaning sweet, little prince or princess

challah: a loaf of rich white bread, usually braided, eaten by Jewish people on the Sabbath and other holy days

cheder: an elementary Jewish school in which children learn Hebrew and the fundamentals of Judaism

di yesurim: misery, pain, sadness

dreck: trash, rubbish

gaon: a gifted scholar of the Talmud

gelt: money

glik: happiness

Got-tenyu: Dear God

goy: a non-Jewish person

goylem: blockhead

hamantaschen: triangular shaped cookies with a variety of fillings

Hanukkah: an eight-day Jewish festival that usually falls in December; also called the Festival of Lights

havdalah: a Jewish ceremony marking the close of the Sabbath or holy day

Kiddush: a ceremonial blessing of wine or bread in a Jewish home or synagogue on a Sabbath or other holy day

Kislev: the third month of the Jewish calendar

lekache: a leavened honey cake

licht bentschen: recitation of benedictions over lit candles on the Sabbath and other holy days

macher: big shot

mazeltov: congratulations

Megillah: a scroll, especially one containing the Book of Esther

meshuggeneh: crazy, foolish

naches: special joy

oy gevalt: a cry of anguish, suffering, or frustration

paskudnyak: an ugly, revolting, evil person

pe'ye: sidelocks; the locks of hair falling at the side of the face worn by some Jews

Purim: a Jewish holiday celebrating the deliverance of the Jews from the massacre plotted by Haman

Rosh Hashanah: the Jewish New Year, occurring in September or October

schmendrik: ninny

schnook: a stupid or unimportant person

Shabbos: the Sabbath—the seventh day of the week devoted to rest and religious observance

shabbosdik: in the spirit of Shabbos

shadchen: a person who arranges Jewish marriages

sheidel: a traditional woman's wig

shiksa: a non-Jewish girl

shiva: in the Jewish faith, the initial seven days of mourning beginning immediately after burial

shofar: a ram's-horn trumpet blown by the ancient Hebrews in battle or for high religious observances

shtetl: a small Jewish town or village formerly found in Eastern Europe

shul: synagogue

Simchat Torah: a Jewish holiday celebrating the completion of the annual reading of the Torah, the sacred scroll kept in a Jewish synagogue in which the first five books of the Bible are written in Hebrew

sukkah: a booth or shelter with a roof of branches and leaves that is used as a temporary dining or living area during the Jewish festival of Sukkot

Sukkot: a Jewish festival that celebrates the harvest and commemorates the period during which Jews wandered in the wilderness

tsores: troubles, misery

tzitzit: the fringes or tassels worn on traditional clothes by Jewish men as reminders of specific commandments

umetik: lonely, lonesome, sad

veytik: lonely, lonesome, sad

yarmulke: a small, round cap that Jewish men and boys wear on their head, especially during religious services

Yom Kippur: a Jewish holiday that falls ten days after Rosh Hashanah on which Jewish people fast to atone for their sins

~ DISCUSSION QUESTIONS ~

New Language While sitting on a suitcase waiting to be processed at Ellis Island, Zippy writes, "I swear on the blessed memory of my grandmother that a year from now I shall be writing in English." (page 4) *Did Zippy keep her promise to herself? How did she learn English? How difficult do you think it is to learn a new language? What, if anything, helped Zippy learn hers?*

Give It Time After one day in America, Zippy writes, "If this is America I don't like it, not one bit." She adds, "Tovah forbids me to say that I hate it until I have lived here at least two years. She says it is unfair to make up one's mind that quickly." (page 8) *What do you think of Tovah's advice? Given time, did Zippy end up liking America? Discuss times you have made quick judgments or opinions and had to go back and revise them.*

One Lucky Girl? At the end of her first full day in her new home, Zippy writes, "Mama keeps saying how lucky we are." (page 10) *What makes Zippy feel like the family is lucky? What makes her feel like they are not? What is your opinion, are they lucky or not? Give reasons for your answer.*

Big for First Grade When Zippy goes to school she is very upset when she is put in a first-grade class. "This is what they do for immigrant children who don't speak English," she writes. (page 20) *How would you feel if you moved to a foreign country and were put in a first-grade class? Do you think it was right or wrong for school officials to do this? Do you think they had any choice? Why or why not? How does this compare to Zippy's father having to work in a sweatshop in New York even though he was a music teacher in St. Petersburg?*

Mixed-Up Mama After watching the tension grow between her mother and father, Zippy writes, "I have figured out that Mama is truly mixed up." (page 37) *How is Zippy's mother mixed up? What does Zippy propose to do about it? Do you think this is a good proposal? Why or why not? How does the proposal work out?*

The Acting Bug After watching a Yiddish play, Zippy decides she must be an actress. (page 67) *What careers interested Zippy before the theater? Why do you think acting grabbed her attention? Do you think she would be a good actress? Why or why not?*

Tovah's Union When Tovah begins to organize a union, Zippy writes, "Mama is furious. She said unions are for men not women. A woman who joins a union will never get married." (page 81) *What do you think of Tovah's desire to start a union? Is it a good or bad*

idea? *Do you agree with Mama that unions are for men and not women? Do you think there is any truth to Mama's belief that a woman who joins a union will never get married? Where do you think she would get an idea like that?*

Big Dreams After Zippy tells Miriam her secret dream of wanting to be an actress, Miriam says, "What is it about this country that makes one dream such big dreams?" (page 88) *How would you answer Miriam's question? Do you think this country still makes people dream big dreams? Why or why not? Do you have any big dreams you'd like to share?*

Matchmaker Zippy's mother sent for the matchmaker to arrange a marriage for Tovah. (page 103) *How does Tovah feel about the matchmaker? How does she manage to send the woman away? How does this make Tovah's mother feel? What does this event represent about life in America for recent immigrants like the Feldmans?*

Miriam and Sean When Miriam and Sean get married, Zippy's mother acts as if Miriam has died. Zippy does not like this. "I have come to be angry with Mama . . . . I do not approve of what Miriam did, but she is not dead. She is in love . . . ." (page 113) *Why does Zippy's mother act as if Miriam has died? What do you think of Zippy's analysis of the situation? How do you think you would have felt in Zippy's shoes? Mrs. Feldman's shoes? Miriam's shoes?*

A Proud Vote Thinking about election day, Zippy writes, "We Feldmans shall all walk proudly down Orchard Street to the polls, even though only Uncle Moishe can vote. Oh, how I wish the Tsar could see us now." (page 137) *Why is voting so important to Zippy and her family? How important is it to you and your family?*

Fatal Fire Zippy's friend Mamie was killed when she plunged to her death trying to escape a fire in the factory where she worked. She and many others could not leave by the doors, which were kept locked so that workers couldn't go home early. (pages 139–140) *Why was this fire such a tragedy? What does it say about the way some employers treated their employees? What role did Tovah and her union have in preventing another such tragedy?*

Happy Reunion When Miriam and Sean come to see Zippy's first performance, Uncle Schmully tells them they must come back to Orchard Street. "We must stop all this nonsense," he says. "Life is too short." (page 150) *Why do you think this was such a happy reunion? What recent events put Miriam's marriage to Sean in perspective? Are there any ways in which you might put Uncle Schmully's advice to good use, by forgetting a long-held grudge, for example?*

~ ACTIVITIES ~

Tanta Fruma's Proverbs Have students decide which of Tanta Fruma's proverbs they especially like. (See pages 16, 17, 21, 39, 49, 54, 81, and 151.) Ask each child to copy the proverb at the top of a sheet of paper and write a short skit in which that proverb is used. Share the skits with the class.

Russian Composers Try to get recordings of music by some of the Russian composers mentioned in the book—Tchaikovsky, Glinka, Stravinsky, Sibelius, Schumann, Rachmaninoff, and Dvorák—and play them for your class. Encourage students to research the life of a composer whose music they particularly enjoy.

Queen Esther Ask students to write about the story of Queen Esther and to make a cover illustration for their work. Share these stories with other students as well as other classes.

"Star" Verbs Zippy writes, "I love that Americans take a noun like 'star' and turn it into a verb!" (page 116) Divide students into groups and tell them they will have a set amount of time to brainstorm a list of nouns that are also used as verbs. At the end of the given time, the group with the most correct verbs wins.

Tsar Nicholas Have students research Tsar Nicholas, the man about whom Uncle Schmully says, "I think there is a point where stupidity can become evil, and yes, the Tsar reached that point many years ago. He is now evil." (page 129) After they have completed their research, ask students to use what they learned to write a short essay evaluating Uncle Schmully's comment.

Answers for Words of Welcome
I. B 2. A 3. R 4. T 5. H 6. O 7. L 8. D 9. I Bonus: BARTHOLDI

Attached to the Earth

In 1903, the year Zippy and her family came to America, the following words were inscribed on a bronze plaque on the pedestal of the Statue of Liberty. This poem, written by American poet Emma Lazarus in 1883, reads:

The New Colossus

Not like the brazen giant of Greek fame,
With conquering limbs astride from land to land;
Here at our sea-washed, sunset gates shall stand
A mighty woman with a torch, whose flame
Is the imprisoned lightning, and her name
Mother of Exiles. From her beacon-hand
Glows world-wide welcome; her mild eyes command
The air-bridged harbor that twin cities frame.
"Keep, ancient lands, your storied pomp!" cries she
With silent lips. "Give me your tired, your poor,
Your huddled masses yearning to breathe free,
The wretched refuse of your teeming shore.
Send these, the homeless, tempest-tost to me.
I lift my lamp beside the golden door!"

After reading the poem, match each word below to its correct meaning.

1. colossus

2. astride

3. exiles

4. beacon

5. huddled

6. yearning

7. wretched

8. refuse

9. tempest

T. a light or fire used as a signal

I. a violent storm

A. with a leg on either side

O. wishing or longing for something very strongly

D. the worthless or useless part of something

R. people sent away from their own country

B. a giant statue

L. miserable or unfortunate

H. crowded together

Bonus: Write the letters on the lines to spell out the name of the French sculptor who designed the Statue of Liberty:

Frederic Auguste ___ ___ ___ ___ ___ ___ ___ ___ ___
                   1   2   3   4   5   6   7   8   9

Immigration

Tying It All Together

❋ DISCUSSION ❋

One at a Time How were Mary Driscoll and Zippy Feldman able to afford to go to America?

"Our only hope" In what way was America the only hope for the Driscolls and the Feldmans? What happened to those who stayed behind?

Discrimination in a Democracy? Who faced more discrimination upon coming to America, Mary Driscoll or Zippy Feldman? Why do you think that was? When Zippy saw a sign that said, IRISH NEED NOT APPLY, she wrote, "It seems sad to see such a sign in this country, which is supposed to be a democracy." (pages 30–31) Do you agree with Zippy that such a sign seemed out of place in America? Explain your answer.

Hard Work What were working conditions like for Mary and other Irish immigrants? What were they like for Zippy's father, sisters, and other Jewish immigrants? Why were conditions so harsh? Why did the immigrants accept such working conditions?

Tenements and Shantytowns What was life like for immigrants in America? In what ways were Mary Driscoll's and Zippy Feldman's living conditions better than in the old country? In what ways were they worse?

❋ ACTIVITIES ❋

Oral History Have each student interview someone who has immigrated to America and share their interviews with the class.

Ellis Island Divide students into small groups and ask each one to research something about Ellis Island. One group can research statistics (e.g., the years it operated; the number of immigrants that passed through), another can find out about the layout of the buildings and how immigrants were "processed," and yet another group can read some actual stories of immigrants who came through Ellis Island. When the groups have completed their research, ask them to share what they've learned with the class.

Moving Photos Kathryn Lasky writes in the "Historical Note" of Dreams in the Golden Country, "When photojournalists like Lewis Hine and Jacob Riis documented the squalid conditions of poor immigrants, there was a public outcry demanding something be done to improve living standards." Encourage students to look through newspapers and magazines until they find a photo that moves them to want to take action. Ask them to write a paragraph describing several ways in which the picture has inspired them. Then have them share the photo and their work with their classmates.

Additional Resources

The following titles, which take place during the time periods studied in *Teaching With Dear America Books*, are part of the Dear America and My Name Is America series published by Scholastic.

Dear America

A Line in the Sand: The Alamo Diary of Lucinda Lawrence, Gonzales, Texas, 1836 by Sherry Garland

Valley of the Moon: The Diary of María Rosalia de Milagros, Sonoma Valley, Alta California, 1846 by Sherry Garland

Seeds of Hope: The Gold Rush Diary of Susanna Fairchild, California Territory, 1849 by Kristiana Gregory

A Picture of Freedom: The Diary of Clotee, a Slave Girl, Belmont Plantation, Virginia, 1859 by Patricia McKissack

A Light in the Storm: The Civil War Diary of Amelia Martin, Fenwick Island, Delaware, 1861 by Karen Hesse

The Great Railroad Race: The Diary of Libby West, Utah Territory, 1868 by Kristiana Gregory

My Heart Is on the Ground: The Diary of Nannie Little Rose, a Sioux Girl, Carlisle Indian School, Pennsylvania, 1880 by Ann Rinaldi

West to a Land of Plenty: The Diary of Teresa Angelino Viscardi, New York to Idaho Territory, 1883 by Jim Murphy

A Coal Miner's Bride: The Diary of Anetka Kaminska, Lattimer, Pennsylvania, 1896 by Susan Campbell Bartoletti

Voyage on the Great Titanic: The Diary of Margaret Ann Brady, R.M.S. Titanic, 1912 by Ellen Emerson White

Color Me Dark: The Diary of Nellie Lee Love, The Great Migration North, Chicago, Illinois, 1919 by Patricia McKissack

My Name Is America

The Journal of Jasper Jonathan Pierce: A Pilgrim Boy, Plymouth, 1620 by Ann Rinaldi

The Journal of Augustus Pelletier: The Lewis & Clark Expedition, 1804 by Kathryn Lasky

The Journal of Jesse Smoke: A Cherokee Boy, the Trail of Tears, 1838 by Joseph Bruchac

The Journal of Wong Ming-Chung: A Chinese Miner, California, 1852 by Laurence Yep

The Journal of Joshua Loper: A Black Cowboy, the Chisholm Trail, 1871 by Walter Dean Myers

The Journal of Otto Peltonen: A Finnish Immigrant, Hibbing, Minnesota, 1905 by William Durbin